MEMOIR OF THE BOBOTES

Joyce Cary was born in 1888 into an old Anglo-Irish family in Londonderry, Ireland. At the age of sixteen he studied painting, first in Edinburgh and then in Paris. From 1909 to 1912 he was at Trinity College, Oxford, where he read law. He then fought, and served in the Red Cross, in the Balkan War of 1912–13. Thereafter, having joined the Colonial Service in 1914, he served in the Nigeria Regiment during the First World War. He was wounded while fighting in the Cameroons, and returned to civil duty in Nigeria in 1917 as a district officer. West Africa became the locale of his early novels. Cary settled in Oxford in 1920, and died there in 1957.

ALSO BY JOYCE CARY

Aissa Saved (1932)
An American Visitor (1933)
The African Witch (1936)
Mister Johnson (1939)
Castle Corner (1938)
A House of Children (1941)
Charley Is My Darling (1940)
Herself Surprised (1941)
To Be a Pilgrim (1942)
The Horse's Mouth (1944)
A Prisoner of Grace (1952)
Except the Lord (1953)
Not Honour More (1955)
The Captive and the Free (1959)
Spring Song (1960)

MEMOIR
OF THE
BOBOTES

Joyce Cary

Illustrations by The Author

Foreword by Walter Allen

**PHOENIX
PRESS**

5 UPPER SAINT MARTIN'S LANE
LONDON
WC2H 9EA

To
Dr. MARTIN LEAKE, v.c., f.r.c.s.

A PHOENIX PRESS PAPERBACK

First published in Great Britain
by Michael Joseph in 1964
This paperback edition published in 2000
by Phoenix Press,
a division of The Orion Publishing Group Ltd,
Orion House, 5 Upper St Martin's Lane,
London WC2H 9EA

A CIP catalogue record for this book
is available from the British Library.

Printed and bound in Great Britain by
Butler & Tanner Ltd, Frome and London

ISBN 1 84212 102 2

CONTENTS

MAPS

ILLUSTRATIONS

FOREWORD

WHEN he went out to Montenegro in October, 1912, to join the First Balkan War, Joyce Cary was within a few weeks of his twenty-fourth birthday and just down from Trinity College, Oxford. "I wanted the experience of war," he told the American critic, Andrew Wright, more than forty years later. "I thought there would be no more wars."

For most of us, later, larger and more devastating wars, in one of which Cary was to fight and be wounded, have practically obliterated any knowledge we may once have had of the First Balkan War—or, for that matter, of the Second, which followed it within a few months and was a struggle over the spoils between the countries victorious in the first. The First Balkan War represented the penultimate stage in the expulsion of the Turks from Europe and was the direct consequence of the seizure of power in Constantinople by the Young Turks in 1909. In England, they were assumed to be good western liberals, but, as H. A. L. Fisher writes in *A History of Europe*:

> All this was the wildest error. The Young Turks were very far from being liberals. The governing force in their movement was a hot and intemperate nationalism. Nothing was more foreign to their notions or to their practice than an attempt to conciliate the Christian peoples. A methodical and centralised tyranny was substituted for the slatternly extortions and numerous massacres of the Hamidian regime. Disorders grew, outrages multiplied. The state of Macedonia with its mixed populations of Bulgars, Greeks, and Serbs, went from bad to worse. New taxes inflamed the Albanians. The union of Crete with Greece was forbidden. In less than two years the harsh government of these Turkish nationalists had achieved a miracle, such as no statesman could have foreseen. A formidable and vigorous Moslem tyranny, led by men who were determined on one last desperate fling for Empire in an adverse world, suddenly healed the feuds of the Balkans and united the Christian populations into a military league.

It was, moreover, a military league that could put 600,000 men in the field, and for the Turks the war, which lasted little more than a year, was disastrous. It was estimated that during the first few weeks alone they lost 200,000 men.

Cary was at the war for six months. As he relates in *Memoir of the Bobotes*, almost immediately after his arrival at Antivari he was arrested as a spy, following an explosion in an arsenal in which he was nearly killed. "Got arrested because I was sitting there when the beastly thing blew up," he told the *Daily Express* man who interviewed him two hours after the event. "Then they let me go when I offered to help the Red Cross." So it was as a member of a British Red Cross unit, indeed as the cook, that he witnessed the campaign described in the *Memoir*.

As one looks back over the course of his life, his sojourn in Montenegro seems wholly in keeping with Cary's character. He was, as he makes plain in *The Case for African Freedom*, a man who took a long time to find himself; a man who,

> after ten years of active, thoughtless and various experience in the world, began, rather late in youth, to ask what it amounted to; to dig up all his foundations, to find out exactly what they were; who discovered then, as you might expect, that some of them were mud, some were hollow caves of air, others sand; and who then slowly and painfully rebuilt them, as far as he could manage the task, as a coherent whole, on which to found a new life and a new mind.

But this period of radical re-assessment of personal values was much later than Cary's Balkan adventure, which belonged to the early years of active, thoughtless and various experience, years that had included, besides his undergraduate days at Oxford, three as an art student in Paris and Edinburgh and vacations spent in Paris with Middleton Murry. Cary himself in his remarks to Andrew Wright seems to me accurately to describe the impression the *Memoir* makes on the reader today, when he says: "... I had a certain romantic enthusiasm for the cause of the Montenegrins; in short I was young and eager for any sort of adventure. I saw most of the fighting and was among the first three over Scutari Bridge, at the surrender of the Turks in 1913. For this campaign I had a little gold medal from the Montenegrin government which I prize very much, though it was earned in what was, for a boy of my age, a holiday."

This sense of adventure and of holiday, of an interlude in the everyday realities of Edwardian England which, for Cary as for the great majority of his countrymen, did not include the possibility of war in which England could be vitally involved, emerges strongly from *Memoir of the Bobotes*, emerges, for example, in the delighted reaction to a novel scene and to picturesque peoples. One may guess that it was one of the reasons, together with the fact that it was not a mature work, why he did not publish it in his lifetime. Just when he wrote it is unknown, but all the evidence indicates that it must have been very soon after his return to England. Cary himself says in his preface: "it is partly taken from a couple of diaries, partly from memoranda of duties, stores required, routes, and so on." Certainly it must have been written at a time when Cary could still assume that prospective readers would have the main facts of the campaign firmly in their heads, for there is no attempt at elucidation of events or explanation of the background to the war. Beyond this, the whole tone of the *Memoir* suggests that it could only have been written before the world war broke out.

This, indeed, is part of its interest for us. It strikes one now as being an intensely pre-1914 document. In a sense, it exists outside the context of our times, as is evident when Cary's attitude towards the experience of war is set against Owen's in his poems and letters, Hemingway's in *In Our Time* and *A Farewell to Arms*, or to that of the writers who took part in the Spanish Civil War or of almost all who fought in the last war. There is, on the one hand, no repudiation of war, no sense of intolerable personal outrage, or, on the other, any passionate identification with a political cause that must defend itself however horrible war may be. The feeling of personal involvement in the action is almost entirely missing, and its place is certainly not taken by Cary's appreciation of the Montenegrin peasantry, who are seen very much as the primitive, unspoiled men and women of the romantic poets. In a word, Cary's attitude towards the scenes he is witnessing is aesthetic. He is at the war as an observer rather than as a participant, as an observer of men and actions essentially remote from him. "My nearest comrade," he says at one stage, "was divided from me by a point of view a thousand years apart"; and elsewhere he writes of the Montenegrins: "For the first time they were fighting by the rules of European warfare and they are not yet enough civilized to know that these rules are never kept." This excursion of Cary's to the Balkan War strikes one now as like nothing so much as a present-day undergraduate's trip in the long vacation to Greenland or the equatorial forests. Rough and tough as it was, it was still a holiday.

This impression the *Memoir* makes of belonging to a time other than ours is reinforced by the nature and style of Cary's occasional reflections, those on food and eating, for example, which remind us that he was writing in the era of the polite literary essay, with its self-conscious flourishes and calculated paradox and whimsicality, the era of Stevenson and Belloc. Which is perhaps merely another way of saying that *Memoir of the Bobotes* is Cary's *Travels with a Donkey* or *Path to Rome*.

Yet, when all is said, *Memoir of the Bobotes* remains a document of great interest, both in its own right and for the light it throws upon its author. It shows that Cary's remarkable objectivity was with him from the beginning, long before he had evolved his philosophy of the creative imagination; and it contains fascinating foreshadowings of at any rate some aspects of his mature work:

> I spent the rest of the afternoon shifting boxes and bales at the Tobacco Monopol (the Italian cigarette Factory, given to us for a base hospital) under the direction of Doctor Bradford, whose chief delight and ruling passion can thus early be seen. He is a man that loves energy for its own sake, and there is no kind of work always so apt to hand in a base camp as the moving and removing of boxes.

Reading such a passage, it is difficult not to see in Dr. Bradford a precursor of Rudbeck, with his passion for making roads, in *Mister Johnson*; just as the sparkling vignettes of characters in action in the same novel seem anticipated by such a description as that of the journalist Count Catapani:

> It would be hard to find a man who was so violently determined to impress—and gave himself to such strange methods of finger-snapping, prancing, moustache-twirling, strutting, now looking down his nose from the full height of five feet six, now brushing an imaginary fly off his shoulder strap, again cocking out his leg, supporting his left elbow on his right hand and patting his cheek with his left, while the polysyllables (accents shaky) flew out of him like ballet dancers with rheumatics.

The *Memoir* helps to define the nature of Cary's objectivity. We are given next to no information, for instance, about his British colleagues in the Red Cross; factually, we learn much more about Gospodin Michan Plomenatz, the interpreter, than we do about Lauder and Doc and the rest. Yet the characters, British and Montenegrins alike, are all unmistakably there, rendered vigorously and economically in characteristic gesture, stance and pose. In this book Cary's function is to be a recording eye, and he is concerned almost exclusively with what his eye sees. As his own excellent sketches to the *Memoir* show, painter and writer were at one in him. His objectivity was a painter's objectivity. The *Memoir* is as it were at once a painter's sketchbook and a painter's notebook.

But the painter was a born writer. Nothing is more admirable in this book than the terseness of the prose, the concentration of description in the fewest possible words, seen at its finest in the splendid conclusion to the narrative, the account of the entry of the Montenegrins into Scutari:

> The generals stopped at the bridge-head for their wine (the chief Turk most violently creased his frock-coat in the effort of lifting the tray high enough) and then rode on.
>
> We ran down and fell in by the standard. At first the course lay through the bazaar, from one small alley to another, covered by the eaves of the houses, which shut out the sky all but a strip of a foot wide. The crowds peered in silence from the dark caverns of the open stalls. Every man and woman of them expected massacre that nightfall, but their attitudes and looks expressed for the most part nothing but indifference made easy by famine ...

Our main interest in *Memoir of the Bobotes* doubtless lies in the fact that Cary was its author and that it is the only thing of his we have that was written in the "active, thoughtless" days before he evolved the philosophy that is the form and being of his novels. Yet if it had come to us as the work of a completely unknown young man of 1913 I think we should still recognise its merits as a record, from a highly individual point of view, of one of the last wars of its kind. That the First Balkan War was, at any rate on the front Cary served on; elsewhere, it seems to have been rather different; from the military standpoint, we are told, the war demonstrated the value of aeroplanes, of which the Bulgarians had a number. But Cary's war was a mountain-peasants' war, and one of the most attractive features of his book is his delineation of the Montenegrin peasant-soldiers, their officers and their families. Cary's appreciation of a way of life simple, dignified and democratic pervades the *Memoir*. It was a pastoral way of life, the sense of which, for Cary, the war never destroyed:

> One had the same impression sometimes on our own Shiroska mountain over Bobote—that it was more easy to fancy the country in deep peace than at war. From the outpost there, high up in clear wind, we used to watch the sheep browsing in Scutari meadows and a shepherd or two sitting under a tree. The line of wire in the plain shone like a stream, it

could be distinguished from water only by its shewing more blue and not changing colour with the sky. The gun emplacements were hidden in clumps of trees, the tents half buried in their pits behind the trench—they suggested at most the Tunbridge Wells cricket week, or a fair. This is not written or pretended for caprice—it is true that, what with the ordinary course of life being by the nature of man to seven-eighths of its consistency invariable and unchanging whatever you do, whether it is eel-fishing, flying, gambling, or polar-exploring, and what with the large indifference of hills,· skies, sun, moon, and stars to small scuffles (the largest battle is small by comparison), it is by an imaginative effort rather than direct realisation that danger and the possibility of bullets can be understood. The sniper waits for·the failure of the imagination and shoots you because you have forgotten that you must believe in him.

WALTER ALLEN

Publisher's Note to Maps

New names, or spellings, have been substituted in recent years for some of the place names used by Cary in this text. Such names appear on the map of the Balkan Peninsula before the War of 1912–1913 (p. 16) and on the map of the Area of the Final Campaign against the Turks, 1912–1913 (p. 87) in the form used by Cary. They are listed below with their current replacements:

Name Used by Cary	Current Name (or Spelling)
Brditza	Brdica
Cattaro	Kotor
Cettinje	Cetinje
Antivari	Stari Bar
Lovchen	Lovćen
Niegush	Njegusi
Scutari	Skodar, Skadar, Skutari
Podgoritza	Podgorica; since 1945, Titograd
Petrovitza	Petrović
Plavnitza	Plavnica

PREFACE

THERE are two ways to go to Montenegro: one by Flushing to Trieste in the through-carriage, from Trieste to Cattaro by the Austrian Lloyd, and from Cattaro to Cettinje by the post-carriage; the other by train to Bari in Italy, and from Bari to Antivari on the Montenegrin coast by the Puglia Company's steamer. I chose the former route and had a very comfortable and prosaic journey as far as Cattaro.

I missed the post at Cattaro, and had to take a cab, which Mr. Hey of the *Daily Mirror* very kindly shared with me.

We drove out in the dusk. A few lacksydaisical dandies were still strolling on the quay and gave the town that look of advanced civilization so much more noticeable in provincial places than capitals—we expected a quiet drive.

But Cattaro stands at the foot of the great mountain of Lovchen strongly fortified by Montenegro. The one road climbs the face of this mountain in a chain of loops and zigzags that make any drive an adventure, with the most sober of coachmen.

Our driver was very young, very gay, and not quite drunk enough to know that the horses were better left to themselves. Galloping in the dark along a narrow road five thousand feet up, with many turns, and nothing but a stone here and there to guard the edge, apart from the magnificent wildness of the hills and the fine taste of the air, was an excellent excitement.

Mr. Hey had a good deal of luggage. There were some memorable times when all this baggage was charging us at once from different corners, while the horses clattered, the carriage swung, the driver howled and lashed; on one side was the wall of the cliff, on the other nothing to be seen but a wisp or two of vapour and a dark pit.

It was like flying, without the easy motion of an aeroplane and its comfortable sensation of balance.

At Niegush they looked at our passports, and we climbed again from Niegush over the mountain wall which surrounds Cettinje. Cettinje itself is in a valley full of plantations and orderly little fields—it is like a small Irish country town in appearance. The Government buildings are exactly like a convent, the Royal Palace like a Court House, the Embassies like a row of small Doctors' and Lawyers', and the Crown Prince's Palace like the local Squire's.

But it is cleaner than any town one ever sees in Ireland, except perhaps Ballinasloe, and it is lighted by electricity.

There is one Hotel, the Grand Hotel, where we fed. We put up in a house opposite, known as the Turkish quarters.

I had hoped to get work with the native Red Cross, because it then seemed unlikely that the British Red Cross would see anything of the war. But after four idle days in Cettinje, I took the advice of the British Minister, the Count de Salis, and of Miss Daubeny, Lady-in-Waiting to the Crown Princess, and decided to go on to Antivari, where the British Red Cross were stationed.

As for the narrative that follows, it is partly taken from a couple of diaries, partly from memoranda of duties, stores required, routes, and so on.

When it refers to Yankees, it means only Montenegrins returned from America, some of them from only a couple of years in the mines, others born in America—but in no case spoken of as typical American citizens.

JOYCE CARY

MEMOIR OF THE BOBOTES

The Balkan Peninsula before the First Balkan War of 1912-1913

Part One

I

ON Friday morning therefore, October 25th, 1912, I took carriage from Cettinje, and we began at once to drive up a mountain. There is no road in all Montenegro that does not go up and down a mountain somewhere in its course, and nine tenths of them are always in the mountains. They are very good roads and would be magnificent for a motorist. You do not get the same outlook from their high soaring loops as in other Highland countries—Ireland, Scotland, Switzerland, or the Tyrol—you do not forget that you are in Montenegro, or by its right name, Tserna Gora, the Black Mountain. The climate is hot in all but the high passes, and the Friday morning was very fine, clear, and sparkling. As we came to the top of the pass between Cettinje valley and the Rjeka Gorge, we were stopped by an old gentleman, who appeared suddenly above the edge of the cliff, apparently out of mid air. He was wearing the ordinary dress of the country, black skull cap, red waistcoat, wide blue breeches, top boots—but he was a very ragged old gentleman. He saluted, gave us good morning, opened the carriage door, got in beside me, and waved to the driver to go on.

He then saluted again and offered me his tobacco box, assuring me it was real Tuzi tobacco. I rolled myself a cigarette, and gave him a ready-made one in return from my own box. In the same way we were stopped by an old woman with a bundle, who was taking her son to the front, and the son, who sat on the box-seat and sang duets with the driver. The Montenegrins are a democratic people, or rather an aristocratic people where there is equality, because all are aristocrats of an equally Good Family. One man has no right to a whole carriage for his own selfish use, nor to a tobacco box, nor to a loaf of bread.

The old man and the old woman started several polite conversations with me, which failed, owing to my lack of Serb. They then discussed me between themselves, and decided I was a Russian, which was a great compliment. The driver was asked and said I was French, which was not so great a compliment, but as far as I could understand, they did not believe him and decided that if I was not Russian I must be nearly related to a Russian.

This driver was much drunker than the man who had brought me from Cattaro, and let the horses manage for themselves, so that we travelled fairly smoothly. Rjeka Gorge, down the side of which the road runs to Rjeka, the first baiting place, was full of small round clouds which moved about beneath us almost at random, as if they had motion of their own; they looked like sheep grazing. Beneath the clouds were strips and triangles of the valley shewing, with terraced farms running up the foot hills like ladders in grey and green, parts of a minute and distant world that seemed as far from us as Atlantis.

We came down below the clouds at ten and shortly afterwards into Rjeka, where we drew up on the quay and got down. The passengers shook hands with me and went off; the driver disappeared into a bar. I had turned myself once about to look for a tobacco booth, when a sturdy paunchy little grey-bearded man in green velveteens and brass buttons, Tyrolese style, rushed at me, and ejaculated half-a-dozen greetings in Servian, in German, in French and English, working my hand up and down meanwhile, as if he hoped to pump confidence out of my mouth.

He was one-armed, his right sleeve was empty, and thrust into the coat pocket on that side, but it was plain that he had been accustomed to clap his acquaintance on the shoulder with one hand while he clasped them with the other, for now he did it alternately, first a shake, and then a clap.

"You are French—you are English?" he asked.

"Irish."

"Ach so. It is the same thing with English. I see your shoes now. English shoes—good. Come and have beer with me. They have the Niksić beer here.* I have seen no sensible person for a week. Excuse me, will you accept of me my card?"

He drew me by force into the Inn and called for beer. I looked at his card and saw he was a Privat Docent from Munich. He spoke very good English in an amazing roaring voice, opening his mouth very wide and turning his tongue over the words in a way that made his smallest talk sound new and forcible.

* Pronounced "Niksitch"; ic is always "itch."

A tall saturnine man, very dark, with a black moustache, came in after five minutes and was presented to me as a friend of the Professor's, Lieutenant Popović, late of the Servian army. He clicked his heels, bowed, shook hands, sat down composedly, and called for beer.

"You are going to Cettinje," said the Professor in the tone of a man who expects to be contradicted.

"No, Antivari. I catch the train at Virpazar."

"To the Red Cross. You are doctor?"

"I am not a doctor. But I am going to the Red Cross."

"The Lieutenant desires very much to go to Antivari. He speaks the language—I am sure he could be of assistance to you—"

"There is plenty of room in my carriage."

The Professor looked very much delighted but at the same time embarrassed.

"Perhaps if you would ask him—invite him. It is rather delicate. He speaks a little French."

I asked the Lieutenant, who accepted, and went to get his bag.

The Professor leant across the table, took me by the lapel of my coat and thanked me.

"I was in distress for him," he said. "He was promised employment at Cettinje, but there were delays and delays, and then they referred him to Antivari. He has found the journey a little dear and his money has not been sent. He is a good fellow, Mister Popović, a good soldier."

I asked why he was not with the Servian army.

"He is an exile," said the Professor. "I do not know the details. I do not press him, naturally. Some of these dynastic troubles, probably the Karageorgević and Obrenović affair, that has exiled many good officers."

"Is he a regicide?"

The Professor was drinking, and before he could set down his mug to reply (he did not hurry to do so) the Lieutenant came back with his luggage and we went to rout the driver out of his den, and post on.

The Professor made me promise to come to Munich and taste his beer. He shook hands a score of times with both of us, and ended by driving out bodkin half a mile, in order to say good-bye again at a turn in the road, from which he could watch our progress for another quarter of an hour.

"Farewell my children," he said to us, when he had got down. "Do not be killed."

Germans abroad are always the most genial and friendly of men. I suppose they miss their domesticity, and try to make new family circles wherever they go, even round a café table, at street corners, in bars. Englishmen pass through the world as if all its countries were so many chambers of the Sarcophagus club, as if they had been only lately elected, and were still afraid of the waiters.

The Professor had united the Lieutenant and myself in his Family, and even after we left him we continued to feel related. Our only common language was French, and neither of us spoke it well, so that we did not converse very much. Probably we had all the more respect for each other in consequence; there was nothing to fall out over. Popović was kindly, resourceful, never out of temper, and these are better qualities in a friend than any amount of talk. We picked up two soldiers on the hill beyond Rjeka, who were travelling the same way. They were both boys of about seventeen, one of them drafted for the first time, the other just recovered of a shrapnel wound in the leg, and going back to his battalion. They behaved at first with the sedate politeness of all their countrymen, exchanged tobacco boxes with us, and talked about the Political Situation, which means in the Balkans always, Austria and Russia. Afterwards they relaxed, fired vollies, sang (in the customary falsetto), and shewed that they were both very pleased to be going on a holiday.

We made a noisy entry into Virpazar. Virpazar is a little island village, or rather it is on an island for the most part of the year, connected to the land only by two long causeways and a bridge. It stands at the head of Scutari Lake, and is joined by railway over the Sutorman Pass to Antivari on the Adriatic coast. This is the only railway in Montenegro. It is of very narrow gauge, the engines are little more modern looking than the Rocket, and the carriages are like horse-tramway-cars. The station stands on the main land, and is a real station with goods-sidings and a bar; the other stations on the line are only huts with a number painted on them.

I made many journeys on this line in the following six months and barely one without incident of some kind—once the steam-pipe burst, once we ran out of fuel and the engine-driver called upon the passengers to go gathering brush-wood with him, again we went off the line, and another time we were snowed up.

This afternoon we got safely over Sutorman, and ran down the loops and twists to Antivari, no more than an hour and a half late.

We could not find any place to sleep in at Antivari. The Hotel was full, and we were turned away from two cottages. A soldier suggested the Turkish prison, where, he said, clean straw had been laid that morning, but he added that it was very crowded. Antivari, or that part of it which is by the bay, does not consist of more than a score of houses all told, an hotel, and a row of wooden huts on the beach.

We dined at last in a two-crown ordinary (a crown = a mark) when we were tired of our search, and decided to ask leave of the landlord to sleep on his balcony. The place was full of officers, however, who at once adopted our interests. The Colonel who sat at the head of the table sent out a messenger with orders to find us quarters. I will have to repeat myself very often if I praise the kindness and politeness of Montenegrins, gentle and simple, whenever praise should be due. These men had never seen us before, and we were not very clean looking—we did not tell them we wished to help their country, because we were neither of us sure of what we would next be at—we were merely strangers, and men doubtful of a bed.

When the boy returned to say there was no room anywhere, they held a sort of enquiry, and examined the landlord, two passers-by summoned with shouts, and each other. Finally a Lieutenant went out to see for himself. We tried to prevent his taking this trouble, but he assured us with a smile that the honour of his country was at stake, and that it was a very cold night, not at all the night for a bivouac without blankets.

He came back in ten minutes to tell us that he had found "at least a roof," and explained to the boy where we were to be taken.

We went off with salutes all round, and followed the boy to the shore, and to the last of the wooden huts. Though there were no lamps it was easy to find this hut because it was full of holes, and let out light itself at every corner.

The three women of the house received us to a ceremonial glass of raki. The room was about ten feet cubed, the original planks patched and criss-crossed in a way that was almost decoration. It was filled very comfortably by ourselves and our tobacco-smoke, bottles and beds and the table, warmed by our breath and the lantern, and aired by gusts of wind that blew the Adriatic almost to the foundations and whistled choruses in the crannies of our walls.

I shared my bed with a longshoreman. It was indeed my own bed

Militza had a kind grave air.

when I first went to sleep, but the longshoreman took up his quarters during the night and moved me politely to one side. There were seven who slept in the room and the women of the house watched us all (except the sailor) to bed. I found this most embarrassing, because I was the only one to undress, and because my pyjamas made such a sensation. They started a discussion and argument which lasted nearly an hour—in the first place to know what they were for, secondly where I had contracted the habit of wearing them, then were they comfortable—and did they not split me in two? Did all Englishmen wear them? Where was England and was it not part of America? Until at last Popović refused to interpret, when they kissed their hands and left us.

2

The women waked us in the morning at seven. They had been up themselves an hour or so I fancy, sitting in the room knitting, and smoking cigarettes.

It gave my first waking thought a hint of the nursery, to be in bed while women sat up gravely and knitted. But I could not watch the sea through the wall of my nursery, and I did through the wall of this hut, by a large crack in the boards just level with my eye.

When I sat up they all said: "Dobro jutro, gospodin," very politely —"Good morning, sir." I thought this a pleasant house to stay at, better than hotels. Popović was half way out of bed—his feet still under the quilt, his hands on the floor, while he gazed between them to find his boots. The young woman who had actually disturbed me, one large hand just withdrawn from my shoulder, stood by. She nodded her head as if to conciliate me and said something I did not understand. She then washed her face in pantomime.

"Dobro bogami (good, bejove)," said I, hastily collecting my pyjamas beneath the bed clothes, and jumping out on the floor.

All the others laughed, nodded, and said: "Dobro, bogami," after me, as if for all the world they had been my aunts, and I four years old. Militza (this was the name of the tall young woman) then brought in a bowl and a jug of water and washed us in the Turkish manner. She poured the water on our hands and necks while we soaped ourselves.

The wind had dropped at dawn but now was rising again, and the hut rocked so that the rays of sun, which shot in at all the crannies, jerked to and fro on the ground, while the sea ran almost to the door. The place was full of salt wind and yellow light. Militza had a kind grave air. She washed us with a serious brow, a dutiful reserve, and then went to make our coffee, while we dressed.

At eight we set out, leaving our bags to Militza. Popović went to the government house, I to the Hotel, to find General Burke, who was in command of the Red Cross.

The Red Cross were still at breakfast, I was told. I sat down in the corridor to wait for them. I had had till then no doubt of being accepted by them. I supposed there was plenty of work to do, and demanded no more than my rations.

A stout white-haired man in khaki came suddenly out of the door just in front of me. He had a long strip of ribbon over his pocket.

I got up and asked for General Burke.

"Yes," he said, "I am General Burke."

I explained myself and what I had come for.

"I am sorry," he replied, fingering his ribbon, "but I can't do anything. You should apply to the headquarters in Victoria Street."

Popović was sitting at a little wooden table in front of our hut drinking raki and smoking a cigarette, when I returned.

"How goes it?" he asked, as I came up.

I was not very pleased to have to tell him I had failed.

"What will you do?" Popović asked. "You cannot live always in this pig-sty. Why don't you come with me to fight?"

I said, "Very well."

"There is the Hague Convention," said the Lieutenant, "but that is all my eye and Betty Martin (I give a free translation)—your mother was a Montenegrin, you were born in America. You can go to the Chefsko-bielitski Battalion; it is full of Americans who speak your language. Or come with me. I am to have a sort of commission in the Lechanski."

I knew that I could pass the governor and the recruiting officer with Popović's help, and so agreed to all he should think fit to do.

We carried our bags at once to the government house, and the governor's wife took them in charge.

The governor was away in Cettinje, and would not return till the evening; so we had the day on our hands. Uniforms were promised for the morrow.

There are two Antivaris, the new town on the coast, the old, some

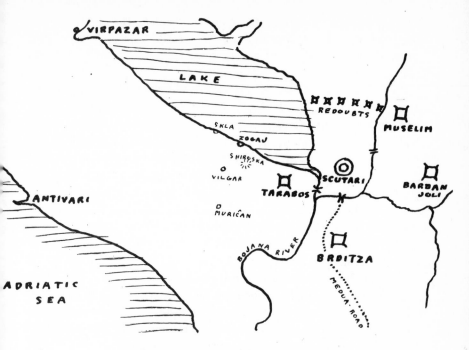

I give a sketch to shew the operations

four miles away, on the foot hills of the mountain. The old town has a
fine citadel of the time of the Venetian power, built in the fifteenth
century, taken by the Turks soon after, and retaken by Montenegro in
the wars of the seventies.

We decided to go and see it. The road lies between wide olive groves.
We walked as far as possible under the trees for shade, and talked about
the chances of the campaign.

Popović told me that the advance by the mountain ridge along the
West side of the lake had been stopped; it was thought the Martinović
division would come to Medua and go up to Scutari from the South,
along the Bojana river. This is in fact what was done. I give a sketch to
shew the operations. We sat in a clearing by the road to understand this,
drawing on the backs of envelopes. Popović, though a figure of mys-
tery, romantic for a novel, was here only a pleasant taciturn companion
in a smashed felt hat, with a drop of sweat on his nose. I looked at

Popović, and fancied him tip-toeing through the dark rooms of that Queen Draga's palace, peering into cupboards and poking his sword through bed curtains. The commonplace infects every person and situation as soon as you are close to them. If the Lieutenant had produced a pistol suddenly, and offered to rob me, there would have been no more than a troublesome brawl, less picturesque than a fight between two sparrows in a gutter or an apache outrage.

I saw an apache outrage once. It started sordidly—a woman knocked down, a man trying to jump on her. It ended sordidly—the woman laughing and running, the man weeping. But newspaper reports of this sort of affair make every city clerk long for romantic outlawry. He takes tram to Poplar and smokes opium, or goes for a gypsy during his week's holiday, and gets harvest bugs in his legs and cannot sleep at night without making his under arm go dead. Real outlawry is no more romantic than a desk.

Antivari-old-town is all on the hill side. Its streets go up on wide steps. It is an Albanian town, full of Albanian men in black and white with tight frieze breeches, and women in orange shawls.

Popović knew the woman of the inn. She was the sister of a Servian soldier killed lately in the Sanjak and they talked about him while we had coffee. Her black clothes brought the war nearer to one's imagination than the levies on the roads and in the train. We ordered cabbage soup for one o'clock before we went on to the citadel.

The citadel can be seen from some miles away. It covers the whole top of a square precipitous rock, like a tower, touching Antivari's hill on one side, so that it is only approachable by one gate. The gate is built in like a guard chamber with a groined roof in stone, and has three openings, one to the town, one to the battlements, one to a flight of steps that lead up higher to a prison.

The place was as dark as a crypt. The guards were squatted smoking round a brazier in the middle of the pavement when we looked in through the bars of the door. Popović rattled the bars, parleyed a few minutes, and we were allowed to pass.

There are fine wide landskips from that height, village, hill, olives, and the Adriatic, and we sat down on a grassy slope between two broken walls to look at them. I suppose we lounged for a quarter of an hour or more.

Then there was an explosion, and we were both rolling down our slope; the shadow of a column of smoke a hundred, two hundred feet high, slid across the grass.

I sat where I had fallen, half twisted round, and gazed at this column of smoke. I remember it had a narrow waist and a very large head. Popović seized me by the neck and dragged me under a wall.

Immediately tons of stone fell, stones weighing a hundredweight apiece slanting down like rain; a box of cartridges volleyed off, and a whole shell went somersaulting over the edge of the cliff in front of us. The stones had already stopped falling and the box of cartridges was exhausted—this shell performed its trick in a moment of silence, passing with a gay sparkle out of the shade of the smoke into the sunlight.

We stood up under the wall. Popović was fingering his moustache and looking at the smoke, now detached and moving off to become an ordinary round cloud.

I began to take out a pipe, but put it back again, as if caught in an impropriety. The pause was uncomfortable.

I noticed blood on the Lieutenant's wrist and lifted his arm to look at it. He paid no attention, but repeated the same sentence three or four times in German.

I said in French, "I speak no German," and he answered, "They will be suspicious."

We began to walk away towards the far end of the mountain top. The fire was now getting hold of the ruins of the magazine, and there were all the sounds of a battle going on at a hundred yards range. Shrapnel began to clatter about us.

I pointed out that there was no way out of the fort except by the gate and that our best plan was to return as innocently as possible—or at least to be returning when captured.

We stopped under the doorway of a tower, whose outer wall was fallen, and arrived at the edge of the precipice as I said this. There was a fall of a hundred and fifty feet. I dusted Popović's coat and made my own more tidy. We found our wind also, for in spite of little exertion we were both panting.

We turned to go back, and were not more than ten steps advanced, when a soldier came jumping over the stones and seized us each by an arm. He was a little man, and his teeth were chattering as he pushed at us. We were in no hurry and made our own pace, for we had agreed to arrive cool. We refused therefore to run when we reached the smoke and dust towards the gate, in spite of the little man's furious indignation, though I don't think he was so much afraid of the shrapnel, as still entirely overset by the surprise of the first bang. His eyes were popping out with excitement, and his breathing was like that of an old asthmatic.

All that I could at first be aware of at the gate was a number of excited soldiers running to and fro in the twilight of the arches, with fixed bayonets; a great crowd struggling and shouting in the street beyond the gate; and a terrible sound of screaming from the dark opening that led to the steps of the prison.

The captain interrogated our soldier, and we were set against the wall by the door from the fort, with an old fellow in a torn uniform to watch us. This man had his head tied up. A thin stream of blood trickled down his nose, and dripped into his grey moustache. But he was perfectly detached and grave, as most Montenegrins are when they are wounded, and did not seem to have any more than a bystander's interest in the confusion.

I asked to see his wound, but was refused. He offered me his tobacco box, however, and opened a desultory conversation with Popović.

We were in a good position at the corner of the inner door. On one hand we could watch the shells bursting; on the other, the row in the gate-house. I could now see that here the screaming came from a great crowd of Mallissori prisoners, Albanian rebels, who had run down the steps from their prison above (I suppose the explosion had burst it open) and were held back at the bottom by a wooden gate, like a cow-gate, across the upper door.

Four or five soldiers were threatening them with their bayonets—they were in no more danger where they were than anyone else.

Also I saw a few other wounded, a man limping, another lying down against the wall, one or two with their heads tied up; Popović said that it was thought there had been sixteen men in or about the magazine when it blew up, and that five only had come back to the gate-house, all hit.

Everyone but the officer, who was dignified but quite bewildered, appeared to have lost their nerve.

About this time a small boy in a white fez wriggled through the gate from the prison, and appeared in the middle of us, looking gravely pleased with himself.

The suddenness of his escape was too much for the soldiers; two or three rushed at him and began kicking him toward the door.

A kick with a soft hide shoe is not of course very sore, and the small boy took his punishment pretty coolly, stopping and looking back between the kicks.

The captain interfered after a moment, pleased to have something definite to do, took the child by the ear, and led him to the gate—I saw him go strolling away down the street with his hands clasped behind him. I noticed too that the street was empty and that the riot was over, while the Mallissori prisoners inside, as if in sympathy, had ceased from their noise. The only sounds were the blowing up of shells and the rattle of cartridges, which never paused for a moment.

Officials began to arrive after the first half hour, governors, secretaries, captains, about half a dozen in all, and all of them questioned Popović, whose explanations tended to get shorter and angrier at each asking, while I confined myself to a declaration that I knew nothing about anything—in French. Then the Red Cross came up, dressed one or two heads, were told that there was nothing more to be done, and went away to find places to watch from.

A few minutes later, two of them returned, and approached the inner door, by which we were standing. These two were Williams and Baverstock, both veterans of the African war.

Williams was swearing very heartily at the bystanders, as he pushed through.

"What is it?" I asked, when he got to the doorway.

"There's somebody inside," he said. "They've heard shouts."

I interpreted this to Popović, who nodded his head to me and said that of course shouts had been heard.

I asked Williams to wait a minute till a guide could be got, and then I would come with him.

The ruins about the magazine are very confused and difficult to find a way in, and I knew a guide would be wanted for the first part of the journey. I saw a captain near me who had already spoken to me in French; so I called out to him in that language and told him what I wanted. He hesitated a moment, spoke to another officer, and then cried out in Servian to the general crowd.

A soldier stepped out and answered, and the captain waved him towards me. I recognised one of two I had picked up near Virpazar in the carriage—he smiled and saluted. The four of us then ran out into the sun, Williams, Baverstock, the soldier, and myself.

Some other soldiers followed us at a distance, and we could see them dodging along behind whenever we stopped to take cover and catch our breath.

I suppose one has a pretty confused impression of all such affairs—of smoke, dust, heat, noise, and a breathless hurry over uneven piles of stones and tumbling walls, one part of you saying, "This is luck," and another, "Damn the shrapnel."

We were taking cover for the last time, to get breath for the last rush, when Williams said suddenly:

"Look at that, Joe!" and pointed down.

Joe Baverstock and I looked, and noticed something like a piece of withered branch with the bark on. I picked it up and saw that it was a man's arm, the fingers blown away at the palm.

"I expect that's the lad that did it," was Joe's comment; I handed the arm to our guide, who put it in his belt.

Then we stepped over the wall and made directly for the fire, up a kind of broad-paved alley.

The smoke was thick, but we tumbled over our man almost at once. He was lying in the open, white as a miller with dust from head to foot; his face might have been cast in plaster of Paris, but for his heavy breathing, and a dabble of blood about the mouth. We dragged him down by the legs until we came to the first wall, where we found a party of the men who had followed us, and handed him over.

As we were going back, a more than commonly loud explosion with a shower of shrapnel (the shrapnel was worse than all the rest together) drove us into a side alley for cover, and we found a second man, entirely helpless and unconscious.

When we had hauled him also down to the bearers, we decided to go back to the gate-house and send for a dresser.

We found however that Ford and Carter of the Red Cross, nursing orderlies, had already taken charge of the first man, as soon as he was brought in.

We knew our way better and made a second journey with much less falling and delay, although we could not find any more wounded.

We went this time upon the ruins of the casemate itself, to inspect a large hole which Williams had spied out among the smoke, but an explosion in that very hole, which had at that range the effect of sheet lightning, both shewed that no one could be alive there and drove us to cover.

Williams was very nearly killed by a splinter in this adventure, and we were all very glad to be satisfied that no one alive was left, and go away. I asked the captain on our return if Popović and I were still under arrest?

He said "No," to me at once, and to Popović after another short parley, of which he took notes in a manner that shewed them to be no more than a form.

It was past two o'clock by now; we were hungry, and went straight to the inn for our soup.

3

I was given a lift back to the new town in the carriage of three of the correspondents, Macguire of the *Telegraph*, Courlander of the *Express*, and Lymbery.

All the Albanians of old Antivari had run out into the olive woods, both for fear of the shells and because they knew they were suspected of treachery. The riot I had seen in the streets immediately after the first explosion was started by a fight between loyal townspeople and the Turkish party, who had been chased away.

Albanian men wear white for the most part, with black braid on their breeches and coats, and sometimes a short black shawl; while the women and children (except those of the Mallissori tribes) go in bright colours; they made a very handsome show, grouped together in families, or moving slowly about among the trees.

I went to the Hotel as soon as we arrived, and ordered a bottle of beer, which I was drinking in the smoking room with a great deal of pleasure, when Doctor Bradford and Doctor Leake, of the Red Cross, came in.

Doctor Bradford asked if I would still like to join them, and I said, "Yes."

I spent the rest of the afternoon shifting boxes and bales at the Tobacco Monopol (the Italian cigarette Factory, given to us for a base hospital) under the direction of Doctor Bradford, whose chief delight and ruling passion can thus early be seen. He is a man that loves energy for its own sake, and there is no kind of work always so apt to hand in a base camp as the moving and removing of boxes.

One ward was already open, an immense high bare room on the second storey, with rows of tall windows, forty gimcrack iron beds round the walls, and two long tables down the middle—the one for bottles and dressings and scissors and spirit lamps and a bandage roller, the other piled with tin plates, and cups, and spoons, and forks.

I went down in the evening to the hut. It was full of longshoremen drinking and smoking, while Popović was sitting on his bed. I was received with many greetings. Militza brought raki and coffee, and rolled me a cigarette. I sat down beside the Lieutenant. He told me his uniform was to be down by the next evening and that he was going forward at once, he was sorry I had deserted him. I was sorry also. I said good-bye with the sense of saying good-bye to many possible adventures; shook hands with the women, and walked soberly up the hill.

The dressers and orderlies slept at Antivari in the annexe of the hotel. I was given a mattress and quilt on the floor of one of the rooms, and went early to bed.

This night I had no pipe or tobacco and was too shy of the others in the neighbouring rooms to ask for it. I lit a cigarette, which is always a miserable compromise at any time, and in bed a nuisance—before I could turn twice over, it had set fire to the quilt.

The quilt was an oblong of stout wadding with a sheet sewn to the inside, the ordinary bedclothes of the country, full of dry rot and dust.

It burnt very fast. I found that stamping not only did not put it out, but singed my feet. I was forced at last to drag it into the corridor and pour a couple of buckets of water over it, of course disclosing my trouble to all the world, a world that laughed unsympathetically and offered very ribald and useless advice.

This was a fine end for the adventurer in his carriage of the morning. I lay at last in the bed of Dobson, a dresser who was away at Rjeka, without pipe or cigarette, or even a silent grin for the other occupant of my room, whom I heard exclaiming down the passage about eleven o'clock, with indignation, "They've put the bl——y orderly in with me!"

4

The next morning I went to the Monopol to learn my business. I had fancied it would be pretty intricate—everyone regards other people's business as rather difficult. A clergyman once told me privately that he could not understand how a boat could be sailed against the wind. I told him that I should be very diffident of attempting his trade, while he declared it required less wits than any other—that that was why the clergy wore their collars back before, as a warning that special allowance should be made for them by ordinary intelligent persons. But this was told me in confidence, and by an Irish parson.

Joe Baverstock had a certain solemn air about him too, when I handed myself over to him for teaching, which made me feel humble and attentive.

I was shewn how to sprinkle the floor in neat patterns, and sweep—how to make a bed by the R.A.M.C. rule, and how to look active and engrossed when there was nothing to do at all. I drew water and fetched basins by the light of nature. Bandage-rerolling is not difficult, and I learnt something of the art of bandaging itself, by keeping my eyes open—Carter shewed me how to make dressings, hot or dry. In two days I was an adept, yawning as I strolled up to duty, unless it was relief duty. Relief duty was duty as Dinner orderly, releasing the orderlies of the day for lunch, and feeding the patients.

There were two Dinner orderlies. We came on at twelve, and the others ceased at once to feign any more interest in broom handles and bed pans, and wriggled into their coats, and stumped off to the Hotel.

First we would toss up who should go into the den of lions. I mean the Sergeant-Major's kitchen, representing (by a legitimate figure) the Sergeant-Major to be equal to several lions.

The kitchen was fitted in between the back wall of the hospital and the mountain-side; an ordinary cap-kitchen with a brick trench for the fire, on which stood pots and kettles as big as washing-tubs.

There were two ways to it, one round the whole hospital, the other by the store-room window.

I went by the window on this first occasion, I did not catch the Sergeant-Major's eye till I was already in the air; even then I made a despairing apologetic grab at the sill.

The Sergeant-Major had four Turkish orderlies, Constantinople, Fresh Meat, Lobscouse and another, who stood and grinned while their commanding officer told me how I should behave. The Sergeant-Major was really a kind man, but I had not yet discovered that no bolts ever flew out of his thunder—he had an immense pot-stick in his hand with which he used to mark his points, and I was ready to dodge at any moment. The smiles of the Turks took off his attention in the middle of the peroration, he made a half turn, the four faces suddenly collapsed upon themselves like burst balloons, and his terrible intonation of "Now THEN!" was addressed to a row of busy backs.

The stew was ladled out of its dixie into a broad flat pan. "If that doesn't satisfy 'em," was the Sergeant-Major's formula as he banged on the lid again and wiped his hands, "why it ought to—Now THEN!" (to Lobscouse with a swift right about) "where's that wood—WOOD —CHOP-CHOP—can't you understand English—cut along young feller, and if they want more, there's more for 'em."

The other orderly upstairs meanwhile cut the bread—hacked down a regiment of loaves as large as mill wheels with a knife like a scimitar, poured the coffee from a pot as tall as a small church into cups like baths, and stood by spoon in hand for the arrival of the stew. The patients were always greatly enlivened by these preparations, and twisted themselves into the most astonishing attitudes in the efforts of watching. There is nothing so delightful as busy and active work which has some sort of immediate result, everyone likes cutting down trees, painting fences, rummaging box-rooms, excavating pits, blasting rocks. If there is a generous touch about it, as in tree-felling or blasting, all the better. So that it was very satisfactory work feeding the ward at Antivari; we were furiously alive for a while, ladling, dividing, pouring with a lavish disregard of quantities ("plenty more for 'em" as the Sergeant-Major said) and could look round at nearly forty good results when the bout of exercise was over.

5

As Popović had told me, the Eastern division under Martinović stopped their advance on Scutari by way of the lake, left two or three battalions to maintain the positions, and came down across the plains to Medua. The Lake of Scutari is entirely surrounded by high mountains, although in one place, just north of the town, there is a broad alluvial shelf.

Vukotić with the Western divisions had reached this shelf early in the war, after battles at Tuzi and Detčić. In both, losses were heavy owing to the rush tactics of the Montenegrins, but, in both, a far superior force of Turks was captured.

On that side, the Turks were now driven back to the mountain positions of great and small Bardanjoli and Musselim. Hasan Riza Bey was constructing his great line of wire and redoubts across the plain between Musselim and the water, to finish the complete ring of defence.

Martinović, who was advancing along the other shore, drove the Turks from the ridge as far as the Shiroska mountain, within four miles of the town, in one long intermittent fight. The infantry outran the guns as usual, and were unsupported. They charged recklessly over the mountain side, and there were a great many more killed than was necessary—the army was inexperienced. The Turks had a tug on the lake, and mounted a gun in her. They were able to steam up and down the shore, and fire pretty much as they liked.

The King ordered the advance to be stopped at the Shiroska mountain, on account of the loss.

Beyond Shiroska, on the same ridge, are the great Turkish forts of Big and Little Tarabos. These were built some years before, but they were not so strong then as Hasan Riza made them during the next two or three months.

If Martinović had been allowed to go on he might have taken Tarabos* then, and finished the war.

As it was, an outpost was put on Shiroska, and a battery below it on the lake shore in front of Zogaj village, while Muričan, a parallel hill about four thousand metres from Tarabos, was taken for a big-gun position. A daily bombardment was started, and Martinović took his division to Medua, to come to Scutari from the south by way of the Bojana river.

There was a race for Medua. The Servians wanted it for a port, and sent a detachment of cavalry. They came through a roadless country of rocks and mountains by forced marches; most of the horses died, and they had three hundred sick.

* Pronounced "Tarabosh."

The Montenegrins got to Medua first. Doctor Leake was with Martinović at the time and saw the entry of the Servians. He said they were an army of skeletons. Two months later these men were scarcely recovered of the cold, starvation, and dysentery. For five days they had lived on apples.

The first field party left Antivari at the beginning of November, about five days after I joined.

They were Doctor Leake, V.C., Lauder, Todd, Warden, and Williams.

I was on night duty when Lauder came down to the Monopol to collect stores for his expedition; we passed most of the night sitting by the table-lantern in the middle of the ward, talking and smoking. Lauder had spent seven months with the Turks, in the Tripoli war, before he signed on for Montenegro, and had many stories of the other side—of night caravans in the desert; of villages that are built in great dug-out pits to be shaded from the sun; of the gun smugglers from Algeria; of the Italians' method of attack, by which with four hours' bombardment they were accustomed to warn the Turks to bring up their regulars to the point of danger; of their airships, and the moral effect of the sound of their propellers.

Now and again I made my rounds with a lantern—our tales were punctuated by the sighs and gasps of the dark ward.

Several women, wives, sisters and daughters, slept here and there between the beds. They used to start up (but silently) from the floor as I approached, partly to help, if I wished to do anything for their patient, partly in a kind of sympathy, to shew that they were also watching—we murmured a greeting as my light caught their patient dark faces, and they lay down again in their blankets.

Lauder generally said, "Bejove, I must go for those stores," when I came back with the lantern, and then began another story.

At four I waked Ford, the other night-orderly, pulled off my rubber jack-boots, rolled myself in a blanket, and fell asleep at one eye-shutting.

Lauder went off to pack his stores. I got up at half past six to sweep. After that, we washed all the hands and faces, tidied the beds, began to take temperatures, and made an important bustle to impress ourselves. The orderlies of the day came on at eight and we went off to breakfast. Lauder I found still at work in the great corridor, passing from one bleak store room to another with sacks and boxes. He commissioned me to get him six Turks, as I passed the prison, and send them up for porters.

6

Dobson, whose bed I used, had been sent to spy out the land at Rjeka, where there was a pettifogging intermediate hospital, run by a native chemist. Rjeka would be important when fighting began again on the lake, because it was the lake port for both Cettinje and Podgoritza, where the base hospitals of the Bohemians and the Italians were, as well as the Montenegrins' own hospital under Matanović.

Dobson saw what could be done, placated and outflanked the chemist, and then came down to Antivari for an orderly and stores.

I was cast for the duty, but stores could not be spared.

Four of us went to the train in the morning, Doctor Bradford (now in command; the General had gone to Servia), Dobson, Joe Baverstock, and myself.

The carriages were full of soldiers except the first, and that was full of women. There were sixteen or seventeen wives, mothers, grandmothers, daughters, everyone with a pack and an umbrella, the four of us, a Servian aeroplane man, and a returned Yankee. We steamed off in bright sun and started upon the interminable windings of the six thousand feet ascent to Sutorman. The soldiers fired out of the windows, Joe and I ate bread and onions, and the commanding officer chaffed the oldest of the grandmothers, to her immense delight and the pleasure of the whole company.

After two hours it got very cold, and in three we ran into a blizzard of snow. The engine made hard trouble of this, and stopped. We got up steam and charged fifty yards, then stopped again.

Sometimes we jumped down and forced our way ahead to look at the drifts. Below one could see the patterns of many thousand fields, marked out with dark lines, a red roof or two like drops of blood, and the black sea.

Down there the snow had stopped, and there were flecks of pale lemon-coloured sun upon it, but with us it was driving like fury, up to the knee at the shallowest; the wind was full of whirls and eddies, but as strong as a rapid. It was delightful to clamber back on the platform of the carriage again, and dive into the warm breath of those seventeen cheerful women (the aeroplane man was polite, but as gloomy as a head-waiter. I heard of his death at Barbalushi in the next month), and stamp and beat one's ribs.

"Ne dobro, gospodin," (no good, sir) cried all the women, accommodating themselves to our small vocabulary.

"Mnogo zima, bogami," was the proper reply (very much cold, by God).

I had a nest of my own on top of a pile of baggage, shared with an old mother, who had no corners. She was above stays, and even the point of her elbow was comfortably soft. When she laughed her whole surface waved in ripples; to make a remark to her was as if you should drop a stone in milk.

Meanwhile there was no food, but plenty of raki—it did not go to the women's heads, good honest people, but it made the Yankee crazy.

He began to quarrel, and since nobody of our carriage would take him up, he tried the soldiers in the next. He started screaming, cursing, threatening blood and death, and dancing upon his companions. Since the floor was as full as the seats, he could not help this if he insisted on dancing, but after he had kicked and bruised two or three of us, and talked loudly of shooting (his enemies were now quite imaginary—the soldiers treated him with contempt after the first two or three passages —I don't know whom he meant to shoot) Joe and I were told to put him down.

He understood the order before we could wriggle out of our several corners. He made a whirling rush across two or three of the women who were sitting on the floor. This brought him opposite my tower and I jumped all fours on him. Joe reached him from the back at the same moment and the fight was over at that one crash.

He gave a terrific howl, hammered the air—and collapsed into himself like an opera hat.

For a moment we were afraid he was smashed in, but there was no harm done. He prayed for forgiveness, vomited, and went to sleep.

The train stuck altogether on the summit of the pass, and we knew it would stay there for the night. The women, whose patience and good-humour were as comforting as a hot dinner and an arm-chair for all of us, curled up together, the younger in the arms of the mothers, and fell asleep.

We turned out to give them a clear field and found a railway hut to sleep in. The door was broken and there was no glass in the windows, but we spent a good night—Doctor Bradford in his own sack; Joe tumbled in with me. Joe is a broad man, and I suppose if we had both taken a deep breath at the same time we would have burst the sack, but we slept well. We waked up powdered with snow and pretty cold in the face, but lively. We were all in hearty good spirits; the outlook seemed to cover half the world, but I don't remember that we were pleased with it for more than a minute; the air was the distillation of air, the inside of the wind, but not near so good to the taste as hot drink, if we had had it. We were probably in good spirits because if we had not been, our hands and feet would have been cold past bearing and our stomachs too empty to be borne.

We dug the engine out between us. The soldiers could not come out in the deep snow because their soft shoes would first have soaked, and then frozen. Joe made a fire in the hut meanwhile, and found a cottage near, almost buried in drift, where coffee could be had.

I have no doubt we would at this day be living on Sutorman, with a bath (hot and cold), a putting green, a motor pit, electric light, and an evening newspaper, all contrived by Joe, if the relief engine hadn't steamed up about ten o'clock, amid volleys of rifle shots, and towed us down to Virpazar.

We found there a boat full of wounded for Rjeka. We had just time to make friends with the Governor, who speaks English (Jesus Christ—pleased to see you, sir) and eat a great deal of fried meat, before he left.

7

We came to Rjeka in the twilight. It is an old town, long and narrow, on a shelf between the mountain side and the river; the houses are as much of wood as stone and have nearly all of them the open second storey, which is the Albanian way of building.

The Hospital had been the Guard House of the Palace. It was a two-storied building, high up on the hill, with a long flight of steps to it; there were two long dormitories, a small antechamber below, with a stone hearth, and a captain's room over it, which we used for a surgery.

Ogilvie and Dobson were in charge of it. Ogilvie was a volunteer from Guy's who had come out with his own stores. The bandages and dressings he had given to Doctor Matanović of the Montenegrin base Hospital at Cettinje, but the drugs he brought on to Rjeka, and Rjeka was practically kept by them for the first weeks.

We were busy in Rjeka, especially the two dressers, but it was not the kind of business that I could like.

I was fomenter-in-chief, and fomenting is dull work. I dressed also a few of the out-patients—an old woman with a carbuncle on her wrist, a young girl with a bullet wound in the back (she had been at Zogaj with her brother), and two Turk prisoners with sore feet, who were more amusing.

A Princess came in now and again to look round, at which times I hid. I had met the Crown Princess in Cettinje—a polite woman with a great wish to talk intelligently in one's own language, which was very embarrassing. I believe she was a Mecklenburg-Strelitz, and so, I suppose, a cousin of Queen Mary's, and a double loyalty was therefore owed to her; but I believe that all the Royal Family ever saw of me was a pair of dirty boots projecting, and a cloud of tobacco issuing, out of a certain private recess in the consulting room, where we kept a camp bed and were accustomed to repose ourselves whenever there was an interval between fomentations.

We took our meals at an inn, the great Jové's. Jové is a small pale woman, anxious looking, and never well. Her house was built out over the water, and I daresay it was unhealthy. But she treated us as if it was our constitutions that were of the most delicate and required cosseting, as if we were thoughtless small boys who had not yet found out how much it is necessary to eat, to face the hard world. I have often come out from supper at Jové's, from—say, macaroni soup, two eggs, the meat that had made the soup, then fried meat, rice and sour milk, three pieces of Rahat Loucoum, and half a loaf of corn bread, all washed down by four tumblers of wine and a cup of coffee, yet leaving Jové dissatisfied with my appetite, and sadly shaking her head. Jové's mother lived with her, a poor old body, very lame, but with an astonishing hiccough. An hiccough is always more embarrassing to other people than to the hiccougher, like the conjurer's failures, or accidents at table, throwing quails about, spilling wine, dashing potatoes upon the floor, or pouring soup into the bosoms of young women—these are troublesome enough to oneself but worse for the general company. This old lady could hiccough louder than a cock-crow, and more suddenly than a gun, but after the first start and confusion, we always endeavoured to pretend that nothing had happened. The Baba herself generally went into the other room—I suspect she put her head under a pillow by the muffled sounds that came out of it.

The work was intermittent; sometimes we were crowded out of doors—and again empty.

We all went fishing in idle times. Jové's stood by the river, and so did the post office next door, with balconies over the water. We kept our rods (young willow boughs) in Jové's and got our bait there, generally raw meat. If Jové was long in her kitchen, between courses at lunch, we ran out and had a cast. The fish looked like bream, or what they call brazers in Lough Foyle. We had a long discussion upon the healthiness of fish in relation to their food. We knew what these fish ate by the places in which the fattest were wont to lie. After all, as Dobson said, "pigs eat" . . . We gave the fish to Jové to cook; she stewed them; and we swallowed the hot dirty water and bones that resulted out of compliment to Jové.

There were small incidents—drunken guardsmen trying to kidnap the nurses; a storm that blew the roof off; a man sent up on suspicion of cholera, and kept under guard of fixed bayonets until he could produce satisfactory and durable evidence that it was not cholera. But this latter I missed.

For all the friendly people of Rjeka and the pleasant look of the town (which would set up a tourist with a lifetime of reminiscence at one visit) I was glad to be out of it when at last I fell ill, and was sent back to Antivari. Not that I liked Antivari any more than anybody likes a basetown. But I knew that any expeditions to the front would have to start from there, and that in Rjeka one might stay (as Dobson stayed) and serve out pills, and boil hot dressings to put on second-hand botched wounds, and eat too much at Jové's, and sleep only by help of opium (it is an unhealthy place) for ever, till one rotted with impatience or took to resignation and the philosophy of Doctor Pangloss.

8

I took post-carriage to Virpazar, train to Antivari, and messed that night with Joe and the rest in the Monopol.

There was little changed, except that the orderlies now lived altogether in the Hospital and that the nurses had come.

The two stories of the Monopol are each about twenty-five feet high, and the whole air of the place, the long dark corridors, with vast doors opening into dim chambers piled with strange looking packages and enormous boxes, the tall large room in which we slept—in spite of Khaki, and heavy boots, and English swearing—was that of a Maeterlinck tragedy. I never waked up in the night to turn over without this impression, not at all weakened by the snores from the beds about.

The muffled step of the orderly in the ward above, the dark high arches through which his lantern could be seen approaching when he came for the relief, should have been incidents in some play of unsatisfied love, perplexed kings, disgraced heroes, poison and slow murder, even if the opening words were, as commonly:

"Now then, now then, shew a leg there, tumble up, you fellers, it's half past six."

My return fell opportunely on the eve of an arrival of stores, three truck loads of heavy boxes, so that Doctor Bradford was in the best of humours.

Starkie had already dosed me, and I was held fit for casual duty.

I was able to throw some of the lighter boxes off the higher trucks with such tremendous crashes, as to ensure myself for promotion. With one I very nearly crushed the commanding officer himself, but he jumped his long legs out of the way with the most manifest delight on his shrewd countenance—there was no doubt in his mind that something was being done, and going forward with shouts, dust, noise, sweating, staggering, ordering, hauling, plenty of hard breathing and hard words, good for the lungs, arms, legs, backs and appetites of one doctor, two dressers, half a dozen orderlies, and half a score of Turks. No wonder he liked it; so did we, and went to our tea with the pride of working men. But I suspect that it was because of that box and the noise I made with it, that I was chosen after four days to go to Virpazar with Starkie.

Starkie did as well in Virpazar as a man can, who has two rooms full of lousy beds, one pannier of medical stores, and no patients, to make a hospital of. It was a credit to him—and pleasant for both of us to think how tidy it was, when we sat out on the rocks of a morning, smoking our pipes, watching the boats come up the shores of the lake to market, and listening for the guns at Tarabos.

Each day we had the same rule—breakfast, the mountain road, the rocks, two or three pipes, the market (to buy figs or chestnuts) and lunch. At one or so we went to meet the train, expecting wounded on their way to Rjeka. We stayed for half an hour to watch (just as in small sea-side villages with one daily boat the whole populace goes to the pier for it) and talk to any English or French-speaking soldiers, drank a coffee with the governor (Jesus Christ, no news, nudding) and returned to the rocks, pipes, and contemplation of that matchless still lake.

On December 5th the round was broken by an order to get boat transport for a second field-party from Antivari. We were at once in a flutter—Starkie spent the rest of the day at the telephone, while I walked up and down outside the post-office door, and tried to follow his diplomacies, by the occasional ejaculations I could hear.

After negotiations with governors here and governors there, with Minister Ramadanović, and Captain the other-one, Starkie was promised a steamer for twelve o'clock on the morrow; he sent the news to Antivari; and we passed the evening, and dined and smoked and went to bed, full of nothing but the hopes of glory. The party came up the next day at one o'clock. There were Doctors Bradford and Goldsmith, Dresser Warden, and Sergeant-Major and orderlies Baverstock, Davey, and James.

"Where's the boat, Starkie?" demanded Doctor Bradford, while I jumped into a luggage-van to see Joe, and to run away from that very question.

Starkie was compelled to admit that no boat had come. But he declared that there was a very good lunch preparing, and hustled the whole party to soup.

Then I came out of the van, and joined him; we ran to find the governor.

We found him in the market, looking, as usual, as if he had just murdered his grandmother and was trying to forget it. We asked why the boat had not come?

"No come?" said he, wagging his fair moustache at us, "Jesus Christ, no."

"Why not?"

"I doan know, no next day, perhaps."

But we had learnt to include the difficulties of this governor, the various swamps, bogs, thickets, and blind alleys of his character, among the ordinary and natural obstacles of Montenegrin travelling, with the doubtfulness of weather, the uncertainty of floods, the scarcity of boats, the steepness of mountains, the cursedness of mules, and the contrariety of pack-saddles. We murmured something about there damn well having to be a boat, or we'd let Martinović hear about him, and returned anxiously to lunch.

The boat did in the end arrive on the next afternoon. She was the petrol launch, so small as almost entirely to disappear when the baggage was aboard her.

But we got into our pea-jackets (British warms), chose our nests among the boxes and the sacks, lit our pipes, and sailed away very pleasantly.

I could write at length, if you would like it, on the pleasures of travelling in war-time, with baggage, and it would all be in superlatives—this situation was most damnable, these mules were the miserablest of all the world, the roads most cursedly rough, the luck never so hard, that night was perfect, the pipe unforgettable, the stew beyond fancy, one camp would be in Paradise, and the next in the hell below the bottomless hell where they put Robert of Shurland, for kicking the monk with his best top boots.

Boat and waggon transport is nearly all a delight—the packing done and the work over at the start, then smoke, talk, plenty of friends, reflection, changing sights, and new country always ahead.

But with pack beasts, the view is the unchanging view of the hind-quarters of a mule and the slipping ropes of a bad pack saddle, the country ahead is lost in the stony track of the present, the friends are in a bad temper, and there is no breath for a pipe—the only reflection is that even the longest day must have a night at the far end of it.

9

Zogaj is a straggling Albanian village on the lake side of Tarabos ridge. It housed the outposts on that side, as Bobote and Vilgar did on the other.

It was dark when we came up, or indeed we would not have come so far, because the Turks were always ready to fire at any boats within range.

Doctor Bradford caught sight of the mosque as we passed (the landing-place is further along the shore) and decided to take it for the hospital.

While then he was parleying with the Commandant Gurnić, and the Sergeant-Major was building a camp kitchen out of tombstones, Joe and I were left to bring up the stores.

It was now quite dark. In front was the rocky mountain side, and a crowd of soldiers (scarcely distinguishable except when they moved, and that was seldom) sitting among the stones of the beach, and watching our furious energies (plain enough to them against the silver coloured water) as we waded splashing in the shallows, fighting with panniers and bags, as if they were alive and could be intimidated by rough usages.

We had found a big Albanian galley in the bay and threw everything into her. When all was tallied, we climbed in ourselves and gave the word *haidé* (go).

The boatmen put out their sweeps, some standing and pushing the loom, others sitting to pull, none keeping any time, but rowing nevertheless very quietly; the boat moved easily down the shore.

A few strokes brought us into sight of the Sergeant-Major's fire, shining on the white wall of the mosque, whose gallery windows already shewed a candle or two.

We passed the pots up first, and the kitchen stores, then back to scrambling and hauling among the rocks, breathlessly abusing the dark, the bad footing, the cold, and the wet.

We supped on the altar to the sound of Turkish mausers. They were far up the hill beyond the outpost, but nevertheless inspirited us. The mauser of course makes a report that is always distinguishable from that of other rifles—it sounds like a double shot.

After supper I went to sit on a gravestone and smoke and look at the water, when a tall figure in a military cloak came to a halt before me, saluted, and said, "Monsieur Cary."

I jumped up and recognised Popović. He was in lieutenant's uniform. We strolled off towards the Brigadier's house, where he brought me to the great kitchen for coffee.

10

We kept the mosque for a hospital, and chose the next house to it, about two hundred yards up the hill, to live in.

Mosques are always good to seize upon, because they are clean, high, and pretty solid. The Zogaj mosque was better than the common run in small villages. It had a neat minaret with a green pointed roof; all the woodwork inside was painted and fretted, and the gallery was broad and well floored. The pulpit we burnt to keep the patients warm, for nearly all the firewood had already been cut down by the troops; there was only enough standing timber, mostly olive, to give cover to the camp.

I was made house-orderly on the first morning, and sent off after breakfast with six soldiers to clean the house.

Meanwhile some fifty out-patients had come in from the camp and were sitting smoking on the shore-path outside the mosque, so that the dressers began also to be busy.

My men stacked their rifles on the balcony and set to work with all the haphazard good nature of the private soldier everywhere, when the weather is good, and the task not too hard.

I suppose we had been at it three hours, so that it was about two o'clock, when there was a sudden rattle of musketry at the top of the hill, and the report of two or three shells.

I was at the back of the house. My men were gone before I could get to the steps—they grabbed their rifles and ran hard towards the out-posts.

"Son-of-bitches Turski!" was the only notice I got from a Yankee, shouted below the balcony as I came out on it.

The mosque was in full sight from the balcony—I was astonished to see the fifty sick men who had been lying in various unhappy and painful attitudes the whole morning on the stones of the shore path, also racing furiously away, with fixed bayonets.

I picked my way down to the mosque and reported to Doctor Gold-smith, at the same time asking leave to go forward.

The firing was now quickened into a continuous roll, with the loud clap of bursting shrapnel at short intervals. Since it might plainly prove

We came at once upon the body of a Turk (opposite page)

to be more than a skirmish, Warden, James and I were allowed to go on with a surgical haversack.

We made the mistake of aiming directly at the summit of the ridge, since the firing seemed to be there, whereas it proved to be more to the South. The last shot was fired as we came to the top and looked out suddenly and in a moment at the whole Bojana valley, downs, plains, woods, the curves of the river, twenty miles and more, to the sea that shone high up as if on a level with us, of green grey and silver.

The ridge runs from Tarabos to Sutorman, and most of the way is narrow enough to straddle, a foot on each side. One comes upon the top always with surprise. I went back and forward over the mountain at a later time often three times a week, scores of journeys in all, but the suddenness of the achievement each time and the outlook on lake or valley never lost their delight.

We turned towards the outpost and began to walk along the ridge. We came at once upon the body of a Turk, and afterwards many more. They generally lay alone in the open, but at one place there were half a dozen together in a small stone sangar, which had plainly been very long defended, both by the amount of cartridge-cases that lay round each dead man, and the grenade handles. I noticed a tin spoon, by the side of each of these Turks, fallen out of his puttees, where his legs had dwindled. Most of the bodies lacked noses. All sorts of tales have been told of nose cutting—Albanians cut noses, and the Montenegrins used to. They brought them home, as being lighter than the heads, to shew how many Turks they had killed, and possibly to claim a bounty.

But if any nose cutting was done in this war (whatever Miss Durham may say, and I think she would now admit that she was misled) it was the Albanian irregulars who did it.

As for the bodies, it is the birds and the sun that take off the noses. The nose is soft, and offers itself kindly to a beak. The sun easily shrivels it. In the same way the flesh about the mouth goes before the harder skin over the cheek bones, and the stomach before the ribs.

The Albanians cut up the Servian rear, the baggage train and the wounded, in the upper hills, and Colonel Popović executed any he caught without mercy. He is a hard man, but he was dealing with treacherous people.

The Turks murdered the Servian wounded after the Servian defeat at Brditza. They could be seen bayoneting them on the ground, or tangled

48

in the wire. But these Turks were irregulars, and most of them Albanians—they elected to stay in the country after the fall of Scutari.

We stumbled along the ridge till twilight. We were still a quarter of a mile from the outpost, and there had been no more than ordinary sniping. The clouds thickened underneath, and though the wind had fallen, what was left of it—an imperceptible movement—touched us as sharply as if we had been naked.

We came down in pitch dark with many falls, cooeeing to each other to find the way.

Doctor Bradford had left that morning by the launch, so that Doctor Goldsmith was now in command; we messed together silently in the kitchen of the new house, and immediately went to bed. Warden, Starkie, and I had seized upon a little back room to ourselves.

We lay down in our sacks, lit our pipes—and ate spotted-dog. This pudding was a great bond between us, and a deep dark secret. It had been cooked at the base and brought up by Warden as a birthday feast for both of us. But we voted Starkie into the company, and cut three equal slices every evening—fair dinkum and no favour, eating slowly.

II

I was cook's mate at Zogaj, and learnt my duty in a stern school. The kitchen was a dark windowless chamber at the back, stone floored and tiled, with a flat hearth at the side and a bread oven in the corner.

We had as table two of those big painted chests that are made in Scutari, and serve everywhere in Albania for clothes-presses. They stood at the darkest end in the form of an L. The officers sat on the short side, the privates at the long.

In the middle there generally swung a sheep, or half a sheep, easily run into in the evening.

The Sergeant-Major's voice made a fine echo in these close quarters when he was instructing me, or exhorting the two Albanian orderlies, George and Marco. George and Marco spoke only French. Naturally, if one speaks English to a person that only knows French and Albanian, it must be spoken very loud indeed to make him understand.

In the dark of the evening, picking my way among the turbaned gravestones from the mosque, I have heard the echo of the roars in which it was explained to Marco that some firewood was wanted.

49

Marco had been valet in Constantinople to Mr. Marling, at the British Embassy, George a porter—Marco rather too pleasant to be trusted far, George long and saturnine, but with a great air about him. He washed plates and forks in the manner of a nobleman playing at the backwoods, and returned to smoke with me over an evening coffee, and talk high European politics, as if he had it in mind to go back shortly to his palaces.

When in the morning George went about his table laying, while I half-naked stoked the oven, we did not much observe each other. George's look suggested "I am a menial for a moment, but you are also a low fellow. We will meet at the table in our proper leisure." Marco chattered in a petulant manner to both of us. The Sergeant-Major, who lived in a dark and dreadful den up three steps from the kitchen, would break in upon us like the first growl of a thunderstorm.

Eight o'clock brought in the whole of the squadron; the commanding officer thinking out a bad pun, Starkie looking pugilistic, Warden rakishly aloof and extremely unbuttoned, all the rest of us merely hungry, sleepy, critical.

The tale of sick in Zogaj was about fifty out-patients a day, so that everyone was busy. Starkie and Warden had the direct labour—we the indirect labour of feeding the consequent appetites.

12

After five days Warden and I had twelve hours' leave to go to Vilgar on the other slope of the ridge, to pay Doctor Leake's party a visit. They had come up with Martinović's army by way of Luasi, Pentari, and the river. We found them also settled in a mosque, but a mosque which, compared to ours, was as a curate's dog kennel to the bath-room of a Bishop.

Williams and Todd were the only ones in, and they welcomed us to fried meat and a rice pudding. They did not tell us that their lunch had been made for two and intended for a feast.

We were new from plenty at the base-towns and at Zogaj, and knew nothing of what rice pudding and fried meat meant to men who had been living for six weeks on sour bread, stinking goat, and cabbage-water.

We only knew afterwards how starved this party had been.

We sat down therefore before the two medical panniers that made their table and began to eat. Immediately there was a noise outside; we looked towards the darkness about the door, which was shadowed beneath the heavy timbers of the gallery, and Ogilvie appeared.

He might have dropped from Heaven, but Williams plainly had a contrary opinion, and the third chance-comer (who, even while answering our astonishment, kept his eyes on the dixie in the middle of us) sat down, seized a spoon, and plunged it into the pudding; Williams gave a sort of short groan, dropped into the dark corner where his blankets were, and did not appear again till we were done.

Ogilvie had come from Antivari, starting with Lauder, who had lost himself on the way with the two donkeys and all the stores.

Even this news of Lauder, that he had got transport and stores and actually left Antivari, invigorated Todd. He offered the pudding to Ogilvie for a second time, who scraped the bottom.

These seem to be paltry matters for a historical work, but they are after all the most important parts of history, and generally forgotten. No one would have bothered to make history at all but for appetite or, at the lowest, hunger.

Take out the meals of any week of your life, and see what is left of you as a historical character on Saturday evening.

Hilaire Belloc, a spiritual man, went on pilgrimage to Rome, for no reason but the good of his soul; yet you will find in the book he wrote to help others on the best road, that the descriptions of eating and drinking are done better than the prayers.

Williams was fond of rice pudding and had not tasted it for a long time.

As for Todd, he always behaved as if he lived next the Army and Navy stores, or Felix Potin. I have seen him give the only potato we had to an overfed scoundrel of a military attaché, who came in upon us on his way from the Hotel at Antivari to the Hotel at Cettinje, and who probably did not pass a day of his life without eating potatoes, and fried potatoes at that.

After lunch we went to watch the firing.

Vilgari mosque was under the edge of a bluff, which covered it. But a walk of fifty yards brought one to the top of the next rise, by a ruined church, and from that all the positions were in full sight, Shiroska Gora, Muričan, and Tarabos.

Muričan where the Montenegrin guns were, was on the right, Shiroska Gora (the outpost) to the left above, and Tarabos straight ahead down the same ridge.

As the shells passed across Vilgari on their way to and fro between Tarabos and Muričan, the flash could be seen as well as the burst.

This was already the time of the armistice, which was respected far too well by the Montenegrins for their own good.

For the first time they were fighting by the rules of European warfare, and they are not yet enough civilized to know that these rules are never kept.

The Turks did not accept the armistice, and worked every day in their trenches. They knew that they would never be shot at unless they fired first.

They used to sit out on Tarabos in the sun of a morning and smoke a cigarette after their coffee, in full sight of the gunners at Muričan. About nine or ten they went in, and after five minutes or so, the first shell came roaring along the top of the ridge and dropped between the two peaks of Shiroska Gora, where the outpost had their shelters.

Immediately afterwards Muričan put a shell into Tarabos, and after five or six shots on each side, the morning's work was held to be over. The same thing was done again in the afternoon, which completed as a rule the firing for the day.

It was the afternoon bombardment that Warden, Ogilvie, and myself went to see that day. The shells from Muričan made the most astonishing noises as they went over the broken gorges and valleys between the two higher positions; shells in flight make every sort of sound—I have heard them whistle (when approaching), bay like a dog, sob like a thousand Marathon runners in unison, wail like a cat, or roar like an express train (when passing close overhead); but to these ordinary notes, in the case of shooting from Muričan, was added an echo that continued often for a quarter of an hour in the far away hills towards the end of the lake.

On this, the first occasion too that we could see each shot at both ends, the flash as well as the burst, it struck us very sharply how long the shell seemed to be in the air. We saw the flash, and then we heard the report and the loud roaring of echoes, a noise as if the winds were struggling among themselves, with the thin whistle of the shot itself in the middle, which continued apparently as long as one would take to smoke half an inch of cigarette, staring intently at Tarabos the while, until a puff of smoke and dust started up from the Turkish redoubts to mark the hit.

This long wait I found especially strange at a later time when the shells were being fired directly towards us. The whistle can be heard (very thin and sometimes intermittent) a long time before the shot arrives. You have plenty of time to reflect that you can't get out of the way because the way is not certain enough, and that if there is going to be anyone killed, he will have to be killed, and nothing more's to be done.

Part Two

13

AT the end of ten days we were dispersed from Zogaj. Starkie and Warden were ordered to Rjeka and went off the next morning by galley. Ogilvie was to go to Medua, and I with him as his orderly. But at the last moment the plan was changed and I was promoted instead to be cook's mate at Vilgar.

This promotion may have been due to the fact that I had had a washing-day that week in Zogaj, and washed a pair of the Sergeant-major's socks into the shirts of the whole unit from the Principal Medical Officer downwards.

The Zogaj party were already shewing the dandified tendencies which afterwards made them a by-word in the force, and it is possible that the curious mottling of their shirts (there was an astonishing quantity of very powerful dye in those socks) determined them to get rid of me.

14

Vilgar's mosque was in two parts under one roof—a closed room, unceiled, unfloored, narrow and high, with a gallery over the door about twelve feet broad, and an outside extension, which was walled only half-way up, and open for the rest. The roof was supported at this end on wooden posts. The gallery of the inner room was reached by stone steps from the outside.

We had our fire against the side-wall of the open end.

At night when we sat in semicircle round it this wall was in a glow of orange and flame-colour, and the sky behind was blacker and the stars brighter in consequence; we were warm and housed, but in the open air.

The mosque was a lonely place with nothing but rocks, hills, and sky in sight from any side of it. It was cocked up on the flank of a rocky bluff from the main ridge just at the point where the scrub stopped and the bare stones began.

There are two sorts of country in those parts, stony hills and clay hills, and they are sharply divided, either rocks growing nothing but wild sage, if that, and then very sparse, or thickly wooded downs full of bushes, grass, and flowers. There were orchids on Muričan, but not so much as a blade of grass on Vilgar bluff. Below us were rough shrubberies, swamps, pits, and pools, much more forbidding than cliffs. Montenegro itself is stones, stones, stones. It was chosen by those original noble fugitives of Servia, ancestors of the present race, for their refuge, precisely on account of its roughness and barrenness, and it is easy to understand why the Turks have never been able to conquer them these five hundred years. Apart from the difficulty of the ground that recently made even Austria doubtful of her chances should she have to fight there, there is the difference of character, which has come out in this war again.

The Turk has always been like a hedgehog, formidable in defence, and obstinately refusing to give way or admit defeat so long as he is not forced into the open, but slow to advance, very dull at a charge, not enterprising in an attack. It was the same in the fifteenth and fourteenth centuries—he took hundreds of years to conquer an Empire that could have been subdued in a less number of months by vigorous assault.

At Plevna he shewed what he could do as hedgehog, and again at Lule, Burgas and Tckatalja, Adrianople, Janina, and Scutari. But he was always beaten in the open field—rushed off his feet, hustled out of his wits, outmanoeuvred, set and kept a-running without chance to gather himself together and get out his quills.

The Highlanders of Montenegro fought him and beat him by these methods in the old days, the methods that won Killiecrankie under similar conditions.

The Servians and Bulgarians used the same tactics in this war. The Servians were able to finish it before they were winded; the Bulgarians stopped to take breath before Tckatalja, and were not able to get any further. The Montenegrins rushed the camps at Berane, Detčić, Tuzi, Zogaj, took more prisoners than they had men in their whole army, and would probably have rushed Scutari within the month's fighting, if the King had not pulled them up to avoid loss of life.

Doctor Leake, Todd, and Warden were on the field in the fight at Luarsi. That is they were on the field at the beginning of the fight, but the fight travelled at five miles an hour the whole time and could not be kept up with.

The Montenegrins chased as hard as they could till they were tired and night came on, and then stopped to count their prisoners. They liked if possible to take prisoners rather than kill.

One man was brought into Antivari after Luarsi with a sword cut across the face that had extended his mouth from ear to ear. His friends were asked how he had managed to get it. It was explained that he was pursuing a Turk, who proved to have a better pace over the ground than he expected in a Turk. He threw away his rifle therefore, because it was in his way, caught the Turk and was sitting on his chest and taking off his sash to tie him up, when some of the Turk's comrades whom he had passed in the dusk, arrived. One of them was an officer and slashed him across the face with his sword as he ran by. His mouth was decided to have been probably of a medium size, and an opening to correspond was left in the middle of his face by the surgeon. When later he could talk, he boasted that he brought in that Turk after all.

The Turks captured in these first battles were largely from Thracian, Macedonian and Greek levies, the Scutari army was five-sixths Albanian irregulars with three or four Nizami regiments of the best sort as a backbone.

Albanians are much the same kind of men to look at as the Montenegrins, tall, aquiline, spare, tough, and extraordinarily good guerilla or mountain fighters. Both races march over trackless and broken hill country as fast as other people go on the road, and have much more dash for a fight left in them at the end of the day. They are after all brought up like chamois.

The children climb when they go for an airing or drive cows, the farmer climbs about his fields, the old men climb two thousand feet for a gossip with a friend, and go home over the precipices in the dark. Houses stick to hillsides like gulls' nests, and the farms are in terraces above and below them, little oblongs and semicircles of soil stepped one over another and built in with stout walls. The top one is often no more than a few yards square. There is a field beside the road between Niegush and Cettinje, which is the highest of such a flight and no bigger than a tin bath, but it was very clean, lately hoed and built in with a wall as thick as a city's. The farmer that owns this field lives in a house so far down that it looks like a toy—a splash of whitewash.

The ridge between Zogaj and Vilgar or Bobote, was three thousand feet high, very rough going, but a soldier was always ready to carry a sack of stores over it for us, and return to his own camp by the same route within the morning.

All the guns and ammunition were taken up it by hand, the guns partly on litters of tree trunks, partly dragged, the shells on the shoulder. Old men of sixty and young men of sixteen could be met any day on the mountain side with six inch shells weighing seventy or a hundred pounds according to their kind, either shrapnel or common on their backs, and travelling at a rate hard to keep up with.

I was on the ridge one day with a Yankee that often carried sacks for us. He was a very sour fellow, but he was willing to be paid for his work, which caused us to employ him. Two of these shell-bearers passed us, going towards the outpost—an old man with a six inch, a younger man with a three inch, and the two rifles. They shouted "good morning—cold weather" at us from the distance as they passed, in cordial voices. The Yankee had been holding forth to me about the poorness of the land and the ignorance of its inhabitants, having started, as usual on our first setting out, with the question: "How you like dis country? Pretty pore I guess." Now he looked scornfully at the backs of the two and remarked: "Son-of-bitches—always happy and always hungry. Don't know nothin'."

Probably the very rocks and cliffs that keep them hungry, and have kept them independent and self-respecting for so many centuries, give them also the good health, good air, and plenty of exercise, that make them happy.

15

The story they tell to account for their geography (and it is very like a legend often repeated in Connemara) runs like this.

When God was putting the earth together, he began with the clay. It was of course easier to his thumb. When he had finished this first model, he poured the water into the holes he had made for the sea. Lastly he took a sack of stones, and started putting them in here and there wherever he thought they looked best. But the sack was not very strong, and as he was passing over Montenegro, he gave it an accidental jolt and the bottom fell out. God, who was perhaps losing his first enthusiasm as a practical geographer, did not pick up the stones again but exclaimed, "Damn—it's a son-of-a-bitch country anyway," and went home. This was told me by a Yankee, and of course he had a Yankee God, as you can see by his conversation.

Williams was the best getter-up of any man I know; about half past seven he could be heard (he slept next me in the dark den under the gallery) to take two or three deep breaths, and chuckle as if he remembered a joke.

Sometimes he even murmured a recollected joke of the day before, but I think that was only a sort of excuse for the chuckle, if he saw I was awake. Immediately he sat up, scratched his head, kicked his blanket off and his slacks on, stepped into his gum-boots (standing ready upright by the wall) tied his neckerchief (unless he had slept in it, as I generally did), stretched, and made a sudden quiet plunge at the door. I caught a momentary glimpse of cold daylight, of piled packsaddles, and rope, and rifles with bayonets, and sheepskins, and pots, plates, and faggots, with Williams in the middle, hunching his shoulders, gently rubbing his backside with both hands, and looking round for the kettle. The door had a stone slung over it on a rope, to keep it shut.

It closed on Williams, and I fell asleep again, to start up hurriedly on his return with the tea, and grab my shirt.

The tea was poured out and went to stand by each man's head; Williams and I drank ours sitting on the panniers in the middle, solemnly sleepy, as if in church.

The Captain was awake by this time with both eyes closed, Todd asleep with one open, Lauder as dead as a Turk, a lump among dirty blankets. Breakfast was my business—I cut bacon fat into rashers, and bread into slices, under the eye of Williams.

"The bacon's cut, sir," said cook's mate, after half an hour.

Nobody ever seemed to care at all for bacon—they might all be thought to be still asleep, but that the tea had disappeared out of their cups.

I went to look up the frying pan and put a stick or two to the fire. Otherwise I should have been caught—for the Captain, when he seemed most sleepy, suddenly blew up, and went off, with a couple of kicks in his sack, a tremendous stretching, an awful yawn, a violent leaping up and down (called Churning the Stomach—and a piece of chaff for Williams, who is learnéd on exercises for the inside), a loud shouting (called singing, for the benefit of Mike the Interpreter, who declares he would rather hear a spoon on a plate, than the opera) and a spring at boot and breeches.

Breakfast was an unbuttoned meal over the fire.

I held the pan and fried; each man made his own toast, and then extended the slice to me for a rasher, or a dip of fat.

The last man, generally Lauder, toasted a slice for me.

Meanwhile Williams prowled with a dixie in his hand, and wished us all at the devil away from his fire, till the stew should be on.

After breakfast, we buttoned up, and while I rebuilt the fire (the frying fire will not stew), the patients were seen to. There were a dozen or so from the camp or Bobote, with dysentery, fever, coughs, sore feet, stomach aches, old bad wounds, frost bites from the outpost, and nervous fancies, for which latter calomel is the best cure.

I swept—a long business where everything stands on the floor and must be moved, where the floor itself comes away in lumps, and the walls drop mortar, and the rafters flakes of dirt—and then went down the hill to dig leeks with Williams. There were two or three poor little swampy fields among the brushwood below the mosque; I suppose the farmer of them was in some bolt-hole of Scutari bazaar.

This was dirty and bad tempered work, the mud sticky, and the leeks fragile; on leek digging days I was forced to wash.

Todd and I went to the spring together. The spring, like most of them in those parts, was well built in. There was a piece cut out of the hillside the shape of a sugar scoop, floored and walled on sides and back with stone, and the spring ran out of a hole, half way up the back wall. We could take a good shower bath under it, and often did so, when the lice were troublesome.

Lunch was of two courses (unless it was plain stew)—soup, and then the meat the soup was made of; with coffee to come after, fresh roasted and ground by the guard (fine ground as it should be) and taken very sweet.

In the afternoon one marched. Sometimes Williams, sometimes I, stayed in, but the three officers always went out, either to the guns at Muričan, or those of Oblique, or over the ridge to Zogaj to wheedle potatoes and sugar out of the hard hearts there, or to the outpost above, to get a glimpse of Scutari.

The outpost was certainly an outpost; it might have been the last forward station of humanity on the rim of earth—wild men in sheepskins gazing from their crannies in the rocks, a little faint fire hidden here and there, nothing more than red embers, a cold hard wind, as steadily moving as a river, a sky of clouds below, shewing little triangles of the microscopic world between, and another close above—all about, rocks and splinters of rusty shell.

It was inconceivable that there should be any war in such a place but that of man and the wind and the cold, yet you only had to look over the last stone to the left, and bur-r-r, there goes a bullet!

Down again to race with the dark, and the night wind—tea and toast by a roaring fire with bare feet warming on the ashes, and coat and breech unbuttoned—then Williams and I to make a pudding and the rest to doze till dinner, a meal with nothing before it, but the delights of pipe and bed.

17

SCENE: (open end of mosque. Sun slanting across overhead. SOLDIERS in a group by door, all sheepskin, stink, cigarette, and fixed bayonets. DOCTOR LEAKE (Cap), in shirt, hat, and breeches standing by fire, looking at the SOLDIERS. MIKE sitting on a stone poking fire with a bayonet, COOKEE sucking a pipe behind the fire and cleaning the frying pan with a stick)

CAP (pointing to nearest SOLDIER) What's wrong with this one, Mike?

MIKE (without moving from his seat, lifts his head, pokes his cap forward to the root of his nose, fixes the SOLDIER with his eye, and says) Huh?

OLD SOLDIER (Tall thin old man. Long nose. Long moustache, long jaw, long neck, in a sheepskin coat, ragged uniform, and home-made cowhide shoes, hair outwards) I am of the Cettinski battalion, I am very ill. I am in great pain. I see red lights like fire when I walk fast, I have pains all over all my bones, and a big hard ball as heavy as stone in my heart. The day before yesterday when I was carrying a shell (grenat) up to the Shiroska Gora, I sweated so that my forehead was like to burst, and my breath—

CAP   What's he say, Mike?

MIKE   Pains all over.

CAP   Have his bowels moved?

MIKE (after enquiry) Yes, *he say.*

OLD SOLDIER Ask the Captain Doctor to write me a letter for the Commandant Martinović. My stomach feels hard like a board. My grandfather felt the same way and he died from just carrying—

CAP What's all that, Mike?

MIKE Same thing. Pains all over. Pains in stomach.

CAP Tell him to open his shirt.

MIKE Open your shirt.

OLD SOLDIER (while CAP goes over him) I had a brother died of the same thing. He had pains all over and sweated when he went up the mountain.

CAP Tell him to shut up, Mike.

MIKE Don't talk.

CAP (folding up his stethoscope) Calomel. Next man.

NEXT MAN (young, large black moustache, earnest look) Every time I lie down at night the blood rushes up my back, and my hair falls out.

MIKE (hitching up his head in scorn) Every time he lays down, blood rushes up his back and his hair comes out. Damn foolishness.

CAP (with gravity) Have his bowels etc.

MIKE Yes, *he say.*

CAP Five grains quinine. Next man.

VERY OLD BATTERED FELLOW (smoking cigarette) Got sore foot.

MIKE Sore foot.

CAP Tell him to take his sock off.

MIKE Take your sock off.

V.O.F. I can tell the Doctor what it's like. I want something to rub on it.

MIKE No, No, No, take your sock off. The Mister Captain Doctor knows all about your foot. He know what's wrong with your foot. But he wants you to take your sock off, and you've *got* to take your sock off. You come from Virpazar way—don't you? Aren't you one of the Marcović family? Their second cousin, Gospodin Captain Vuko Petrović is a sort of relation of—

CAP What's all this—Mike?

MIKE Won't take sock off.

CAP Then I can't do anything for him.

V.O.F. Vuko Petrović is a fine man. I know him well. His little daughter Maritza is married to my—

61

"But it's rheumatism—I want that stuff you rub—"

MIKE Take your sock off.

  (V.O.F. sits down with resignation, takes off sock, and extends a gangrenous foot, two toes gone, the rest going, with the air of being victimized by medical caprice.)

CAP When did that start?

MIKE When did you get a sore foot?

V.O.F. It went like that after we left Medua. It's all swamps down by Pentari way. My brother had rheumatism just the same.

MIKE Time of Pentari march.

CAP He must go away.

MIKE You must go home.

V.O.F. I can't go home. I'm on duty today. I have a shrapnel standing outside against the wall, to go to the lower mortar on the Shiroska hill.

MIKE Captain Doctor says you must go home—

v.o.f. But it's rheumatism—I want that stuff you rub—like my brother.

MIKE —and so you've *got* to go home.

(CAP, MIKE, O.M. great argument. OLD MAN finally sent off with a tenth cousin who happens to be near, has proved persuadable of the badness of the OLD MAN's case, and promised to deliver him at Zogaj with a letter.)

MIKE He's a good fellow, Captain. I know his mother long time. She was a first cousin of my brother's wife, that woman you saw when you come last home to eat the sponge-cake—nice woman, seven chillun, six boys.

CAP What's this man want?

MIKE (looking at next man) Huh?

MAN (a flagman—young and hard, cap over left eye, clean uniform) I want the milk for my brother. .

MIKE Wants milk for his brother.

CAP Where does he live? We've sent out one tin already this morning.

MIKE Where does he live?

MAN In the second straw house beyond the straw house where Niko Milić lives in Bobote below the bottom stone house, and forty paces beyond the second tree by the stream counting from the well. There's a dead horse just by Niko's house. It's ten paces from Niko's house.

MIKE Son-of-a-bitch mixed up. Send Vuko with him to find the way.

CAP He's the last?

MIKE (to the general group) Any more of ye sick?

CHORUS No, gospodin Michan, came with my father—my second cousin etc. Just came in to warm myself etc.

CAP Well, Mike?

MIKE That's all, Cap.

CAP Then I'll go down to Bobote with this fellow. Cookee, get me a tin of milk, and tell Todd I'm off now, if he wants to come. What are you doing Mike?

MIKE I was just goin' to do a liddle piece of roast meat on this bayonet.

CAP But who's going to interpret for me?

MIKE He's been in Amurka, this man's brudder. He speak English all right. Doan you remember? He's the feller in the red wesket that come in las' week, and you tol' him to go home.

CAP If that's the man why didn't he go home when he was told. He was 103 and a half then. He's nobody but himself to blame if he dies.

MIKE   He's not bad feller, that young feller in the red wesket. He comes from down Niegus part I guess. Cousin of that old feller with the sore foot, good family.

Of course there were usually more patients than this, but these are samples, and all true. The second sounds like a stretcher, but it's not. Todd, Williams, and Lauder can all bear me out.

18

Gospodin Michan Plomeñatz was the interpreter of Vilgar. He was a man of sixty five or more, bent in the shoulder, but strong, handsome, and learned. His learning was all of practical, small matters, cooking, victualling, fire-making, pack-tying—a very good sort of science, and since he could not read, or very little, his memory was sound, and his opinion on immediate matters worth listening to. He went to America in the seventies, mined for a beginning, and kept a saloon afterwards, as most emigrating Southerners do if they can. Now he has a good property there, and lives on its rents. Mike knew us all by his own name. We were to him Tadd, Irish (which did for both Lauder and myself) Mister William and Cap. He also called us his 'chillun.' "Oh! chillun, chillun, what's in that there dixie. It's burnin', fit for a house-a-fire." The dixie was always under his eye, for his appetite was enormous, especially for meat.

The fireside was his place, his home, his occupation, his audience-chamber and judgment seat. There in the morning he brewed his coffee and made his roasts—interpreting meanwhile across his shoulder. He sat there often all afternoon at one of his stews, which were certainly surpassing stews. He was in his corner in the evening to tell stories, and kick the logs into the centre as they burned.

19

Stores came to Vilgar mostly by Katrcol. We sent away one of the guards (we had two a day) or one of the boys who were always attached to us, with a horse, and if luck was in it, he came back after a day with a sheep, a sack of beans, a slab of bacon-fat, a bag of bread, and a bag of rice.

These were army rations.

Our luxuries, coffee, tea, sugar, tinned milk, macaroni, were Red Cross stores, and came to Zogaj by water. We had to fetch them over the ridge.

We carried them over on our backs—Lauder and Todd brought one consignment on the donkeys, George and Mary (George made a reputation for cool-headedness and courage in this affair, which was never forgotten), but Mike, God rest him, the next time we had a rumour of sugar and coffee at Zogaj, advised us to take a pony.

Todd and I believed him, went out one morning, caught a pony, saddled him, and set off up the mountain with a young limb called Vuko Vuko was one of the boys that lived in the mosque and did odd work for his food—he was a short, brown-faced, impudent-eyed, cock-nosed

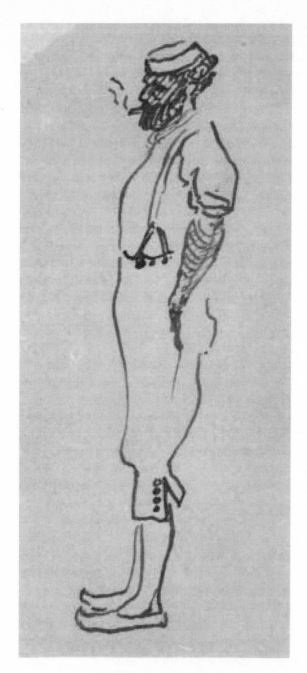

Todd . . . believed him

son of Satan, but never out of humour. He towed the pony by a halter, skipping lively ahead from stone to stone, and yi-yi-ing. Todd and I marched soberly behind in single file, and discussed barbed-wire and bullet-holes, and potatoes, what a difference they made to a stew, or some such grave matter.

We were perfectly contented, as everyone is when he is out on an expedition over mountains, and easy in our minds.

The pony certainly fell down very often, and breathed very hard, while Vuko's screams and yowls plainly discomforted its poor spirits, but—Mike had advised a pony, and Mike was at least sixty years old, an exceedingly wise and handsome old man. We rested at the top as usual, on the edge of the world, looking into the hundred miles of valley on one hand, the twenty miles of lake and mountain on the other, for ten minutes, then began to go down.

The pony fell twice as often, frightening us for its legs, while Vuko nearly pulled its head off with the rope, and howled like forty demons.

Todd and I damned him now and again when we thought of it; for most of the way we fell behind, and discussed sconces, why they had gone out at Trinity, Cambridge (whose Audit Ale should surely have kept the custom alive) while still an every night affair at Trinity, Oxford, with other grave matters. We came into Zogaj with a last shattering fall for the pony, tied the poor beast to the tree in front of the house, gave it a bunch of grass, and went in to lunch.

Vuko was as demure as a young virgin before the Sergeant Major, and ate the meal of an archdeacon with the mouth of a female chorister.

Afterwards we brought out stores into the garden, a box of sugar, another box of coffee, macaroni, tea, a tin jug, two blankets, and the pony seemed to sink one degree in the scale of chevalry at every package—its nose more miserable—its coat more mangy—its knees more knobby and overhung—its belly more pinched, its rump more peaked.

We began to pack—Vuko swearing jaoli (the devil, I spell phonetically) at every tug, and bogami (by God) each time he spat.

He told us the pony could not carry our pack.

Now Mike is a grave honest old gentleman if ever there was one, and we told Vuko to go to blazes, clapped the jug upon the top of the blankets and ordered him to lead on.

There are no roads anywhere in these further parts of Albania, not even in the villages; a sort of stone pathway, very irregularly paved, is the best they can do between house and house. They are dangerous in the dark, and very uncertain even by broad day. It is not surprising therefore that the unhappy pony (who was shod) split itself in two at every step.

I caught its eye in one of these bad moments, and was moved by immediate pity to say very heartily:

"Damn that old villain!"

"What," said Todd, "Mike?"

This was high treason, for it was part of the King's Regulations that everyone should respect Mike Plomenatz, but I repeated it five or six times in different ways as a protest against all Fortune, and in order to harrow Todd; for I was determined to hurt someone, and saw that if I hit the pony, it would probably fall down, and if I assaulted Vuko, he would run away.

We had come now to the worst corner, a place where the causeway turns sharp up the hill in broken steps.

We tried to quiet our beast and then went at it—Vuko made a frightful screech, Todd and I rushed to give the pack a hitch on either side, there was a clatter and a crash and everything was overboard, with the pony kicking on its back and the saddle worked round on its stomach.

A party of soldiers ran out of a ruined cottage to help us. Vuko stood the whole time on the steps and made speeches—one long speech.

We decided to divide the pack—a company flag-man went off to catch another pony, and we sat down on the boxes to smoke.

About thirty men squatted about us, and listened to Vuko's speech. At last one of them remarked in Yankee English:

"Pretty bad road, I guess—bad mountain."

"Very bad for horses"—this by Todd.

"You from Vilgar, I guess."

"Yes—Vilgar mosque."

"Pretty bad place over there."

"We get more sun than you do."

"No fishing-house at Vilgar, no raki, no wine, no tobacco."

"No."

Pause.

"You from England?"

"Yes."

"Two thousand miles and more."

"Amurka's fine country—greates' country in the world."

"I expect it is."

"Shure, sir." Pause. "I get dollar a day in Amurka—don't get dollar a day fightin'. How you like dis country? Pretty pore, I guess."

"We like it very much."

"See that young feller there" (he pointed at a brown-faced young man sitting on a rock with his rifle between his knees). "That young feller's father have five tausan dollar."

The young feller smiled when he saw himself pointed out, got off his rock, saluted, and offered Todd his tobacco box. Todd gravely acknowledged the salute and made himself a cigarette.

"That your boy?" went on the Yankee, who was making conversation out of politeness.

"Yes."

"What's his name?"

"Vuko."

Vuko grinned devilishly at hearing his name.

"He say jus' now he was in the fight at Medua."

"It's a lie—he never was near it—he hasn't got a gun."

"He says he has a gun—over at Vilgar."

We both scowled ferociously at Vuko, and gave him the character of a thief and a liar to the soldiers, who immediately passed the word to Vuko. Vuko was neither displeased nor abashed; he ejaculated, "Né, bogami," and grinned.

The other pony came and we put on the packs—but it is a tale that beats the sad story of Modestine to flinders.

After a journey of one hour, shouting, whacking, tugging, jumping from rock to rock beside the track, and holding the saddles on by main force, sometimes lifting one brute or another bodily out from between the rocks by the girth, we had covered half a mile at most, and gave in.

Vuko thrice damned (I still remember the bursting veins and pouring sweat of that evening) then ran off up with the sugar box—to shew his good will, I suppose. He was of course not strong enough for it—though he swore when we took it from him—the ponies had gone back with the flag-man, and we had to carry that box over in turns.

They received us very calmly at Vilgar—Mike was roasting a row of mutton gobbets and bacon fat (put alternately) on a bayonet, the Captain was sitting with his puttees off and his hat on the back of his head, toasting bread. Harry was stirring the stew, Williams a pudding, the guards smoking, all gaily illuminated by a big fire.

They looked at us with the air of disturbed philosophers—unconscious of other life and disinterested—they said they were pleased to see the sugar, sugar was short, and they wished we had managed the macaroni.

We said nothing, but we saw that Vuko had hot supper. We knew he was a scoundrel, but we knew as well what the mountain was like in the dark.

To tell a story of this Vuko, when the Brigadier Vukotić took over our mosque (on being shelled out of his own house at Bobote) in January, Vuko was thrown in and became his servant. He attended the Brigadier in the February battle.

They were on the ridge in a very hot place, when the Brigadier became thirsty and sent Vuko down for a bottle of wine. Vuko was sprinting off among the shrapnel, when the Brigadier, who was watching thoughtfully his danger, recalled him and told him, when he should be coming back with the wine, to carry it under the *leeside* arm. I believe it arrived quite safely, for I've seen Vuko since, and he was not hit.

20

Before Christmas we sent Vido (the other boy—a good lad) with a horse away to the base at Antivari for any hampers that might have come from home.

In three days Vido returned with four newspapers, two letters, and half a dozen battered oranges. It was decided that Cap, Todd, Lauder, and Mike (they were all sick, and needed a change very badly—while there was little to do at Vilgar for the moment) should go, and leave Williams and me to keep the place.

They went early one morning (about the 22nd) in caravan, Mike riding, and the rest marching, with full haversacks, water-bottles of cold tea, Vido, and a spare pack-horse, for the booty of Antivari. Williams and I enjoyed a perfect holiday in endless lounging.

We spent many hours merely sitting on a stone in the sun, too lazy to look for the burst of the shells even when they were fired, and that was only at long intervals.

We did not do more than the least possible cooking, swept only on alternate days (it was true there was less mess—Lauder and Todd were both away), and I saw the patients, except those that had something wrong with them, who were sent on to Zogaj.

There was an accident one morning which hurt my reputation very much. I had just treated six men (two calomel, two quinine, one dressing for a bullet wound, and a Dover's powder for a cough, to be taken at bedtime)—they were sitting round the fire very contented, and watching me stir the pot, when a Yankee came in.

The Yankee said he was a "little bit sick here," and pointed at his navel.

I recollected the man for a humbug—but told him to sit down a minute.

"Are you doctor or cook?" said the Yankee suspiciously.

"Cook," said I, "but I know what your trouble is. I'll give you something to make you comfortable."

"Where's the doctor?"

"I'm the doctor."

"You said you was cook."

"Can't you see I am a cook just now. I'll doctor you as soon as the pot boils. Have your bowels moved lately?"

"You not doctor?"

"Have your bowels moved lately?"

"Shure, sir—but you not doctor?"

"What's all this about?" asked all the company round the fire in their own language.

The Yankee explained shortly that he had discovered I was a cook. They all got up, their symptoms began to return, and I saw them march off headed by the Yankee for further advice some five miles off.

Not only did my out-patients from the camp decrease in number from that morning, but I think Williams had a poorer opinion of me. He knew already that I was no good at rice puddings and now I had been publicly disgraced as a medical man into the bargain.

On Christmas Eve we became almost sentimental in the hope of reunion, of letters from home, and fresh stores. We made a big stew in the afternoon with more pains than usual to keep it thick and avoid the ordinary flavour of greasy boiled water which is apt to infect goat-stew, but no one came although we waited for some time after dark.

71

We stood at the outer door and watched the Muričan searchlight cross swords with that of the Turks from Tarabos—stab at batteries and glance off mountain-tops into the stars, a very spectacular duel and all in silence—until the night wind began to get up and blow coldly.

Then we went to our dinner and ate the dixie-full between us and fell straight into bed to sleep off the surfeit. It was only a surfeit of quantity, for there is very little hunger satisfaction in goat-broth. It is no exaggeration to say that one had to eat till one was swollen in order to last for a short three hours without growing weak.

Williams is very elastic owing to a long sojourn in the East, where he learnt to eat rice, and did not suffer so much as the rest of us from this necessary tightness, though, possibly for the same reason of elasticity, his figure showed more distortion. Nevertheless Williams' look of repletion was always diffuse, ours more local, exactly the reverse of our respective powers of sleep. Williams had no such thing as a doze—he was either asleep or awake, and the transitions were as sudden as they were complete. We had all learnt to enjoy the middle state, a sort of Buddhist nodding while sitting by the fire, leaning against a wall, or even on a march, and keep our eyes open, our pipes alight, and a look of moderate intelligence on our faces at the same time. George and Mary were excellent models for us. I have seen Mary taking repose in this way with a bunch of grass in her mouth and after twenty minutes or so of brown study, wake at a gun-shot, switch one ear round towards the whistle of the shell, turn the other ear in the same direction at the burst, listen with decreasing interest while the echo died away, her ears slowly falling, discover the grass in her mouth after a moment of ennui, and begin to chew again. Lauder himself could not have behaved with more dignified reserve. Mary was his favourite as George was Todd's and I expect there was a communion of interest and character in both cases. George was deliberate, resourceful, self-contained. Both George and Mary were capable of extraordinary energy on very short commons, if there was need of it, and for the rest were good-natured animals, not looking for difficulties or quarrels, fond of condensed milk on their bread, slightly ramshackle in appearance, as might be expected where combs were so scarce, and tolerant of everything on two legs or four. Certainly there was a communion of character.

We were frying our bread for breakfast on Christmas morning and considering whether it were possible to get enough suet from a goat to

72

William and I were afraid of wounded at Vilgar finding no one there to dress them ...

make a duff, when Lauder walked in. He was bursting with the news of Christmas dinner to be had at Zogaj; had been climbing over the mountains almost from dawn to tell us about it and take us back with him. He had lost Cap's party and did not know where they were, supposed them held up by weather or lack of transport, somewhere about in the hills—somewhere about in the hills was a close description for anybody's situation in Montenegro or Albania.

We saw our patients, made a stew and left it banked in hot ashes for anyone who might come in, thrust a green twig through the ring of the inner door to shew it was not to be opened by strangers, and set out at once.

The Zogaj dinner was the Sergeant-Major's triumph. We had soup, roast meat, a pudding, part of a cake, almonds, chestnuts to remind us of turkey, and cognac with the coffee. The Sergeant-Major was in terrible anxiety over it, which made him so thunderous that we ate in silence and avoided his eye. A spark would have caused an explosion, but the spice of danger added greatly to our pleasure in eating. He smiled at me once when I asked for a second help of meat, but it was a terrible smile.

A heavy bombardment began suddenly just when we reached the pudding and the party broke up quickly as soon as the coffee was swallowed.

Williams and I were afraid of wounded at Vilgar finding no one there to dress them, and left at once, climbing nevertheless very heavily and not stopping until we had reached the summit of the ridge in case resting should make us lazy. We saw nothing there however but a few shells and came down to the mosque at a slower pace.

Williams told me as a great scandal that he had heard that in workhouse duff the proportion of suet to flour was often less than one part in nine. If this is true (but I can scarcely believe it) the government ought certainly to appoint a Duff Inspector under the Weights and Measures Department of the Board of Trade, but it sounds like an exaggeration.

"I don't think the man would have said a thing like that if there hadn't been some sort of truth in it," said Williams just after we had got into our sacks for the night; "he may have been prejudiced of course, but he seemed an honest enough sort of fellow."

On Boxing Day it was wet.

74

Vilgar mosque was a desert island in a boundless sea of wet rocks under a thousand leagues of wet sky; its two Robinson Crusoes gave one look at the dismal solitudes about, then built up the fire, scoured a pan, mixed a mug of flour and water and sat down to make slapjacks.

There are two schools of slapjackers—the epicurean and the stoic, the thick and the thin, the one to please the sense, the other to tickle the taste.

For thin—make a thin mixture, and put very little grease in the pan—for thick, make a thick mixture with plenty of flour, and have a quarter of an inch of fat to fry in. The thick are satisfying but they give you a pain unless you are used to them; the thin settle easily, but leave you hungry.

Williams made them thick—Cap, thin.

We were discussing the pros and cons of slapjacks, while Williams fried, and I was eating the fragments of a failure, when Cap, Todd, and Mike came in, steaming with rain.

They brought a mule load of Christmas stuff with them, a cake from Miss Herbert at Antivari, oranges, a tongue, almonds and raisins, crystallized fruit from home, a pudding from Miss Daubeney at Cettinje, Todd's hamper, and Mike's basket, half-a-dozen letters, and two newspapers.

21

We gave a dinner to the Brigadier Vukotić with these stores. The Brigadier is a big man with a red nose.

"That man's a *bottle*," said Williams, "anyone can see that."

He brought his battalion flag-man with him, one of the finest figures of a man that ever I saw, to be shot to pieces in the February battle.

Each battalion and each company has its flag-man, and every battle sees half of them killed.

It is plainly important in an irregular force, that every man should see at once where he ought to be—so that flags are very necessary.

A Montenegrin battalion on the march (generally in single file owing to the narrowness of the tracks) does not look as if it had much order or discipline, but at every halt it falls into companies.

Large bodies of these troops (for instance, before the entry into Scutari) were managed without any confusion by this system. The flag-

men took their orders and the company followed their flag, the companies their battalion.

A battle was managed in the same way, but each flag-man had to be provided with his deputies, and it was generally a deputy that carried a flag at the end of the fight.

The post is hereditary; it is the flag-man's sons and nephews that wait to take the flag from him when he is hit. At the beginning of the campaign the flags were carried by veterans—at the end by youngsters.

Perhaps it is a good thing for their service, this heavy death-rate, which allows young men to learn their work in each war, who can be expected to last out till the next and hand on the tradition.

However, Vukotić's flag-man was very happy at our dinner, ate a good meal, shook hands even with the cook and the cook's mate (as did also the Brigadier—good honest, democratic fellow) and went away plainly expecting to live as long as any man does when he has just had dinner.

There is little more to say of Vilgar—our excitements were these occasional journeys, caravans, bombardment, searchlights; our pleasures, smoking, talking, the fire, coffee, sleep, and slapjacks; our work, the sick, sweeping, cooking, mending, water-drawing, tree-chopping, fire-making; our advantage, the open air and a free life; our hardship, a shortage of sugar or tobacco, a sore foot (all our boots were burst—Todd and I were both in native slippers), wet clothes, or an increase in the normal force of lice.

We had the pleasure of civilization without the pain, taking it that the pain of that state is all outside, and the pleasure in. Soap and clean shirts are only the binding of the book—useful to keep it together, but paid for with a grudge.

22

About the third or fourth of January, when we were sitting over the fire in the evening, with a storm of rain and wind blowing about the hills and rattling our tiles, Mike was telling again the story of that famous Irish family of the Hickeys, who seem to be very numerous and lively in California; Lauder was boiling up an orange (already thrice boiled on other evenings) in the tea; Todd was dozing with his beard in the air and his cap on his nose; the rest of us were toasting our feet

...we were sitting over the fire in the evening ... (opposite page)

and listening with sleepy admiration to Mike—in fact we were at home, when Dr. Bradford marched in with Warden and told us in his first words that the unit was recalled. Home was blown up under our feet by some polite old gentleman in London, who had never so much as seen a Vilgar fire, met Mike, heard of the Hickeys, eaten roast goat-meat, drunk orange tea as they made it in Tripoli, or conversed with George and Mary in the understandable language of stale bread—an absentee and an evicter.

Cap and Mike went off the next morning. It is easy to break up a household when all the furniture that does not fit into a haversack can be carried by one mule. When we had made their breakfast, packed their beast, and watched them out of sight along the mountain track, we knew there was nothing to be done but follow.

We stayed one day to sort stores—what to take and what to leave—had a last enormous rice pudding so thick with condensed milk that it was as hard as soap, eaten by the light of all the candles left, twenty candles, and wound up with coffee and a smoke, by a fire that nearly set the beams alight.

Dr. Bradford had already gone on to Zogaj to carry the news. The day after the pudding, Warden, Todd, and I met him below one-tree pass by the well, and we marched in together.

Williams and Lauder still lingered on the pretext of taking stores to Zogaj—we left them negotiating for mules, with no great air of being hurried.

The Monopol at Antivari we found in all the miserable confusion of breaking up. It was strange to notice how much we had degenerated now that we compared ourselves to the party at the base. Some of them cleaned their buttons every morning, many washed their faces, all had boots. We had gone down hill together so gently and unanimously that the decline from day to day had not been noticeable.

Our civilization had temporarily separated itself from the general trend, and travelled along different lines—lines of peace rather than a course of struggle. Probably it is necessary for everyone to breathe a certain amount of antagonism in his daily air—housewives wash babies, Chancellors make taxes, and while we had the Turks the Antivari party faced their buttons, and by their own account had much the worst of the choice.

It had been debated already whether or no we should go back to the front, and defy the polite old gentleman, but Cap was away at Cattaro to look at the Austrian mobilization, Ogilvie was at Medua, and Todd had been sent to Rjeka to relieve Dobson.

Meanwhile no news came through from the Zogaj party. But a couple of days before the Bari steamer left, by which the unit was to go, Cap, Ogilvie, and Lauder all came back—we had a conference, saw Dr. Bradford, who said we could do what we liked, but unofficially, and went off by the roundabout route for Vilgar.

All this episode was an anticlimax. We were held up two days at Virpazar for lack of a tug to take us to Skla. We lived at the old mother's in the street by the water-side to the left of the bridge-head—the last house but one (this recorded for the sake of future travellers—the old mother has clean beds) for two days. Mike came down to help us, but failed to bring the tug with all his intrigues. On the third morning he brought his maid Storka with him as a bulwark against our reproaches.

We breakfasted in the street. Storka was a very handsome young woman—she sat herself down gravely and took stock of us. Probably we were the first foreigners or wild barbarians she had ever seen. Lauder attracted her attention at once, and she gazed at him with so much earnest attention, that Mike asked her what she thought of him. She replied with some hesitation, but a real enthusiasm, that Lauder was like the fresh flower of Spring—like a rising sun.

Lauder, whose complexion was burnt to the colour of fire, and whose hair is naturally neither brown nor yellow, but of a happy medium (with a dash of orange) smiled doubtfully at this compliment, and turned the conversation over to me, with the request to Mike to find out "what she thought of Cookee."

Storka looked at me with a critical wrinkling of the corners of her eyes, and made a non-committal reply that might be translated as "pretty fair." I asked if all the people of her village were good-looking?

She understood this innuendo very well, laughed, made her black eyes sparkle and declared that the handsomest women and the bravest men of all Tserna Gora came from that village.

I was casting as powerful a languish into my regard as could be worked up so quickly, and Lauder was watching the effect with approval, when the Governor was spied on the bridge, and our party broke up to chase him. We had a stormy interview and, still in the heat

79

of it, seized a dinghy by force—impressed three quay-loungers for crew, flung our baggage aboard, and set out immediately on the voyage, rowing vigorously away among the tops of the billows. The crew was mutinous, which was not at all astonishing, and looked at one time so disaffected that we divided them—one rowing bow, one at three, one steering, while we took two and stroke. Two were therefore always resting, one of us and one of them (Lauder did not come—he was to go in the first place to help Todd at Rjeka) and the other four at work.

From eleven that morning to eight at night we rowed over a level shining lake, as big as an ocean over the low gunwale of that craft, and past an endless chain of jagged mountains, continued into the sky by even wilder ranges of cloud, with the slowly-moving sun to mark the passing of the day. We worked like mechanical toys after the first few hours, only forced to think when a finger frayed, or a leather slipped off the thole-pin and had to be jerked back by a movement outside the ordinary routine, with a noise different from the regular pull-hearty, pull-hearty, pull-hearty of the sea stroke. We were lost for a while when the dusk fell, and wandered among mysterious islands—all dark, steep, and armed with rocks, until suddenly we came out into open water, and saw the camp-fires of Zogaj with the silhouette of Shiroska and Tarabos for a background.

We touched the wall by the mosque in the pitch dark—our crew bolted for the camp as soon as we set foot on the causeway—finished our boat-stores for supper, and tumbled into our sacks for the night with a feeling of merit. Actually we had done no good for ourselves.

The first thing they told us the next day was that the Brigadier Vuko-tić had been shelled out of his own house in Bobote, and taken Vilgar mosque in its place. He had no doubt spied out the land at that Christmas dinner. Then it began to rain a deluge, and the rain stopped the fighting, and put everyone in a bad temper but Starkie, and a stranger would not have thought Starkie's very good.

They did not want us at Zogaj—Todd and Lauder were not there, or we would have had a strong enough force to make a revolution, seize the house and the magazine of stores, barbecue the commanding officer, poison the patients, and start off with a clean sheet—but, as it was, we were houseless and propertyless dependents, and felt it.

We had no tents, and no house was to be found even if anyone had been brave enough to look in that weather. We were told on every side that the war was done—in short, when a steamer came up one day unexpectedly, relying on the mist for cover, and it had to be decided in a quarter of an hour between staying and going, we made a petulant choice in a hurry, and went.

We came back to Antivari by Virpazar and the train, from Antivari to Bari in Italy; from Bari to Milan and Paris—where we had a bath—to Calais, Dover, London and motor omnibuses.

Part Three

23

THE second party went off on Sunday, February 23. It consisted of Doctors Leake, Sherwin (of the Australian Army Medical Corps), Anderson; Dresser Power; and Zealander and myself, orderlies, who travelled third, looked after the baggage, and played halfpenny nap.

I was now on the strength, with a whole uniform and a kit—no longer to be the tramp, ragamuffin, and outcast of the force.

Apart from the ordinary incidents of sandwiches, lager beer, broken and dream-haunted sleeps, customs, complicated tickets, inquisitive strangers, and an unhappy strike that kept us five anxious days in Bari, there is nothing to be said about the journey. Zealander won fourpence halfpenny and a two sous piece from me in the eight days.

We were rescued out of Bari by special steamer sent from Antivari— the "Antigone," a bad old boat that Greece lent to Montenegro for the war.

Twenty of the Italian Red Cross were on board with us, neat, pompous little men wearing side arms. They were bound for the Italian base hospital at Podgoritza. I suppose their bayonets proved useful for spreading ointment. The "Antigone" took a day and a half to cross the Adriatic. She was nearly as broad as long, and rocked in the dead calm of harbour. At sea she rolled, pitched, checked, jumped, raced, and yawed till St. Nicholas, who lived in a little wooden temple between the stern windows of the coach, with a lamp in front of him, almost bobbed his head off.

We came to Antivari harbour in the dark, and could not get to the pier. I was sent ashore in the jolly-boat for mails. There were no mails, and I sat for an hour and a half on a rock beside the boat waiting for the Greeks of the boat's crew to return.

I could see Militza's cabin further along the beach, letting out rays of light at every crack. At last I went down to it to have some coffee for the cold wind. The place was fogged with smoke and human steam, but round the table were the three sailors with their drinks—two were arguing, the third, a small wizened fellow all jack boots, fur cap and moustache, had Militza on his knee. Militza looked as grave and demure as ever. She was much larger than the Greek. Imagine Miss Constance Collier sitting on the knee of Nietzsche.

She got up to shake hands with me, and went to fetch coffee. The three Greeks all touched their forelocks and sat gazing.

We stumbled across the shingle to the boat as soon as the coffees were drunk. It was rough and we had some difficulty in getting beyond the breakers. Militza stood on the shore and shouted advice, running forward at the ebb of each wave, and retreating hastily when the next ran up the shore.

The "Antigone" was brought in next morning to the pier—the party went to the Hotel, except the orderlies, who stayed for the baggage.

The Italian stores and ours were all tumbled together in the hold by the weather, and we had to sort them, and hoist them, and disembark them, and pack them on a truck, and convey them to the station—it is well known that at such times, all is fair game, and merit is due by results.

We had done a good deal of transport work by now and knew how to begin: first we shook hands with the donkey-man and gave him a plug to put in his cheek. One or two likely-looking A.B.'s also received plugs.

We found two of our old Turk friends on the pier (Constantinople and Fresh Meat) and sent them for others.

When the hatches came off, Zealander took all below decks, I all above; the two A.B.'s under Zealander put only our bales in the sling, the donkey-man allowed time for them to be found, the Turks were waiting, and I had seized the first truck on the quay, a trick that blocked the line, so that none could leave before it.

Meanwhile those dapper little Italians walked up and down frisking their bravo cloaks at each turn, twirling their moustaches, and leaving everything to the stevedores.

They were displeased for a moment when I took possession of the truck, but when I pointed out that my bales had happened to arrive first, they saw the justice of the position and retired.

I stopped three of our cases on the way to the Italian truck, and received their corporal's apologies with gracious indifference (as gracious as it is possible to seem with a very dirty face, a pouring forehead, and an unbuttoned uniform streaked with dust and mud). Of course these cases had British Red Cross painted on them as large as life, but I was glad to see the Italians had made some attempt at piracy; an ill-conceived and poorly managed attempt, but enough to satisfy our consciences that we were not winning a hollow victory over the unresisting. We came to Bari with forty packages, and brought away forty-three from the hold at Antivari, leaving the quay seated on the peak of the pile with such deportment that an old fellow with no seat in his trousers, whom we passed on the way (six Turks shoving behind) sprang to attention with a convulsive start, and saluted in the manner that is usually kept for Brigadiers, and the Prince.

All but Cap and myself, his orderly, went on to Virpazar that afternoon with the luggage.

We had a last polite dinner with beer, filled our haversacks against the morrow, hung them behind the bedroom door, and turned in between sheets.

In the morning we drove as far as the road goes, to Petrovitza on the Montenegrin border, and thence marched for the front.

It is twenty miles of bridle-path, mule-path, goat-track, no path at all over rocks, bogs, streams (but mostly stony hillside), one river, and two considerable high passes to Zogaj. This is the best sort of journey, over an open country with plenty of ups and downs, on foot, finding one's own way and carrying one's own rations, with good wells not far apart, and a clear sky. Cap is a marcher with that sort of spring in the joints which is like wit in an argument.

We had a second meal of chocolate and snow on one-tree pass over Skla and came down to Doctor Goldsmith's quarters at five o'clock.

All who had stayed out were there, Doctor Goldsmith, Todd, Starkie, Lauder, the Sergeant-Major, Williams, and Ford.

Lauder was actually dresser to the Cettinski Battalion over the ridge in Bobote, but he was sick with a poisoned hand and a swollen arm, and they had him at Zogaj to be cured.

I sat on his legs (he was in bed) in the little back room after supper, and smoked a pipe over him, and heard the news.

Meanwhile a council was held by the chiefs, and it was arranged that

84

Cap, Lauder, and myself should form a field unit with its base at Bobote, to go over as soon as Lauder could march.

24

By going away we had missed a battle.

While we had been at Vilgar, a gun-road was cut up the Vilgar side of the Shiroska Mountain, to a shelf below the outpost.

On this shelf three guns were placed, two seven centimetre, and a howitzer of small calibre. These guns were never used. The Turks could have knocked them off their narrow perch in a couple of days if they had been discovered.

They were masked with stones and brushwood, and kept to support an infantry attack.

It is about two thousand five hundred metres from Shiroska Mountain to the Turkish redoubts on Tarabos, but Turkish snipers, under cover of their guns, were able to come within a few hundred yards of the Montenegrin outpost. They kept on the lake side of the ridge (because the Montenegrin guns at Muričan covered the other slope) so that they did not find this masked battery.

In February Scutari was attacked from all sides.

Vukotić to the South-East of the Lake took Great Bardanjoli at the point of the bayonet.

Great Bardanjoli was a very strong position, trenched and wired, on the top of a steep mountain.

He cleared these trenches twice over, for the Turks made a counter attack in the night, and reoccupied them for a few hours.

It was said in Scutari afterwards that a third of the Turkish regulars were killed in that part of the fight.

Hasan Riza Bey knew that the line of redoubts across the plain between Muselim and the lake, and Great Bardanjoli were the weakest parts of his defence. They were weak only in comparison to Tarabos and Brditza, but he expected an attack there.

He kept the best part of his regular regiments in barracks behind these positions, and saw that they had good food, meat, and bread, however the townsmen fared. Each day they were exercised, and did their class firing at the butts. We could hear their shots from Zogaj in December and January for many hours every morning.

Vukotić took Great Bardanjoli only with a heavy loss, and Little Bardanjoli, a position quite as strong, was still in his way. At the same battle the Servians attacked Brditza. The Servians had come to give assistance with a good deal of boasting. In each other part of the war, in Thrace and Macedonia, at Tchatalja, Gallipoli, Adrianople, they had been the saviours. They brought only a couple of thousand men and four light guns to help against Brditza, and were entirely defeated. Some of them got inside the wire only to be murdered at leisure when the rest had been driven off.

The Turks came out afterwards and bayoneted the wounded. Some of them were tangled in the wire, and hung there helpless until they were shot to pieces, or spitted.

Brditza is to the South of the Lake, across the Bojana.

Immediately across the river to the West of the lake starts the Tarabos ridge, first Little Tarabos, then a plateau, then Big Tarabos, the Navel, the Nipple, a long dip, and the Montenegrin outpost.

There were three lines of wire around the Turkish position. One encircling the whole, that is, from Little Tarabos to the Navel, the others round Big Tarabos. When I write encircling, it is not in the strict sense, for none of these lines were closed except the last, that round the fort on Big Tarabos. The outer was open towards Scutari at the back, the second on the inner side.

Martinović unmasked his little battery above Vilgar, and rushed all the Turkish outposts and snipers into the Navel on the first day of the battle. That night maxims were brought to the Nipple to cover an assault.

After a night's fighting the wire was destroyed, and the Navel taken. An attack on the next wire failed. The troops were exposed all day, and got themselves killed with indifference, but the wire could not have been reached even with the loss of half the division. The Japanese in their war have lost ten thousand in charges on such positions and failed.

But the Turks were cleared from the ridge; and Shiroska Mountain, a hill scarcely climbable for a goat, was turned into a gun position.

Of course roads had to be built, and emplacements cut out of the face of the cliff, but when we came back at the end of the month the work was done and there were eleven guns on the mountain.

In this battle, the Red Cross of Zogaj treated all Martinović wounded,

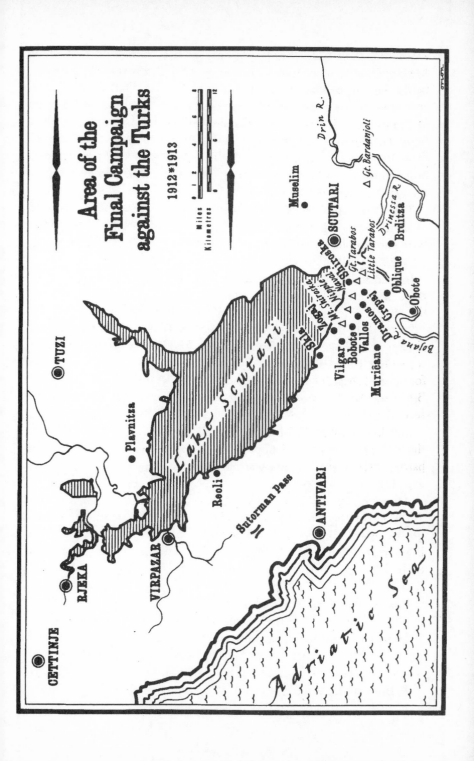

more than five hundred. The wounded would have had two or three days journey to any other help, and half of them must have died.

Todd, Starkie, Lauder, and Williams were all in the field, though the most part of the wounded had to be brought down to the mosque for treatment.

The Montenegrin army has no Red Cross in the proper sense. There is one medical student to each battalion, who is expected to look after the first field work. Of course, these were no good at all, and scarcely pretended to be. They carried swords, and behaved like combatants. There were no stretcher-bearers at all, no doctors nearer than seven miles of almost impassable country from the fighting, and I never met a soldier who had a first field dressing, although they were said to have been served out.

25

I slept that night on the mosque gallery, in a place nicely calculated between Williams' and Ford's beds, the hatchway, the piled boxes of bandages, and the range of the interpreter's spit.

At breakfast Lauder discovered himself in uniform, a ragged and staggering object, but determined to try the mountain. He had to be towed the last thousand feet by the sleeves of his coat, but we ate our lunch on the back of Shiroska Mountain, within sight of Bobote itself.

We were interrupted by the sudden arrival of General Martinović and his staff. The General is a tall man, six feet four and upwards, thin, brown, and in very hard condition.

His manner was the excellent manner of the Montenegrin, eased by an education in Vienna and Paris.

We jumped up and saluted, explaining that we were on our way to Bobote. It was of course the first the general had heard of this, but we knew very well that it is always better to do things in Montenegro and get permission afterwards.

He declared himself very much pleased, reminded Cap of their old times together on the Bojana, told us to apply to the Brigadier Vukotić for quarters, shook hands all round, and rode along up the ridge towards the guns.

... every one steamed, the fire smoked, ... and ... we sat in a fog like that of the Black Hole (opposite page)

Cap followed him as soon as lunch was over, going to see the new gun-roads and the new emplacements on the summit—Lauder and I went down slowly to Bobote.

Bobote is a village about half a mile forward from Vilgar mosque, an irregular ring of cottages round a market-place, all upon a steep slope two thirds way down the mountain. The market-place itself is on an angle of 45, the cottages are all one storey on the upper side, two on the under, with a balcony on the usual plan.

They were all dirty, broken, leaky, cramped, and crowded; the dirtiest, lowest, and meanest was Lauder's and his room the worst in it.

He had lived there a fortnight; a camp-bed in one corner was his retiring place and the rest of the floor was taken up by six or seven soldiers and their rifles, bayonets, baggage, cooking-billies and sheep-skins, with two women (sisters of one of the soldiers), a big flat stone hearth, and a box full of drugs and bandages, all this in a room ten feet by eight.

The billies and cooking pots of the whole party stood about the fire fitted into holes between the sticks and nests in the embers, while the women stirred and the owners watched; every one steamed, the fire smoked, each soldier had his cigarette, and when we were battened down for the night we sat in a fog like that of the Black Hole.

Lauder dropped on his bed as soon as we came in, rolled his blankets round him and slept in his boots.

I lay down with the soldiers—while I had the use of one man's chest for a pillow, another used my thigh; I borrowed a sheepskin from a third for quilt, and slept as deeply as one always does in foul air.

26

One of the men made us coffee for breakfast. Lauder saw four patients (one rheumatism, one cough, one belly-ache, one wound to be redressed) and then we went out to sit in the sun.

The crowd of soldiers that always squatted in Bobote market-place invited us with many tongues to have a drink, but we said it was too early, and made for a quiet place on the mountain side, where we might sleep, or enjoy such conversation as is but one degree from sleep.

We came down the hill at twelve or so and found Cap and Todd in the market with a mule load of stores from Zogaj. The stores were put

The court-martial was held in a straw hut below the village (opposite page)

90

into Lauder's bolt-hole, and we all marched off to Vilgar to see the Brigadier.

We found our old mosque there changed. The outer open part had been walled up with wicker work; there could be no star-gazing by Vukotić's guard while they sat by the fire, and no wind over their heads. But they were veterans of several hard wars, and hated a draught, and loved a big fire, roast meat, snug quarters, plenty of blankets, brandy, and all the home comforts.

Vuko was there too, and danced round us on our first arrival like the young demoniac he was, with many "jaolis" and "bogamis."

The Brigadier told us he would hold a court-martial in Bobote after another hour, and find out what quarters we could have.

We returned meanwhile, and made a lunch of boiled rice and bacon fat.

The court-martial was held in a straw hut below the village. It was a round hut, all roof, lighted only by a big fire in the middle.

The officers sat round in a ring with Vukotić himself opposite the door, an enormous and imposing figure in the fire-light.

We were brought in by an orderly and given our places. Cap next Vukotić, Lauder between Pieter Martinović, Commandant of the Cettinski Battalion in Bobote, and the battalion flag-man, Todd and I alongside each other by the door.

Coffee was made by the Commandant's servant and handed about. The officers rolled us cigarettes, a log was put on the fire, and the first witness called.

I suppose it was actually a sort of Congested Districts Enquiry. I could gather that most of those called up described their houses as exceedingly overcrowded. Cross examination would reduce their first statement of the number of sleepers in a room from fifty perhaps, to fifteen.

When one from each house had been heard Pieter Martinović made a statement, and Vukotić gave judgment. We were to have two rooms in the lowest house and straw huts were to be built for those turned out of them.

The Court then broke up with more cigarette rolling, saluting, and handshaking. The etiquette is two salutes to the handshake—a courtesy-sandwich with the meat in the middle.

The Commandant was already giving his orders in the village, and the first of our rooms was cleared at once. We brought down our baggage to it and set up house. Last we commissioned one Borjo

I had made a neat clean fire ... always a foot or two of spare dry faggot to be urged in ...

Lazaarović, a friend of Lauder's, for interpreter, hung out the flag, and put on a billycan for tea.

27

Our two rooms opened off the gallery of the second storey—to the left the surgery, to the right our own place.

This was a very high square room with a broken floor, and a roof of twisted black rafters. One wall was wicker work. It gave upon the gallery, and we slung a piece of canvas across it for the sake of privacy, but anyone who wanted to look in could always push a hand or bayonet through a chink, and move the cloth to one side.

The back wall had a three-foot hole in it, which was sometimes stopped with a sack, for a while with a board, but generally stood open. It acted as a chimney to the fire in the back room; we got their green smoke and their frizzled bacon all day. A soldier would now and then stick his head through it to ask us how we did.

The third wall was solid and had a shelf upon it which we used for bandages, and a cupboard in it which the mice and rats used for nests. In the fourth were two small windows with wooden shutters, one at each side of the hearth.

Cap slept under the far side window in his wolsey, I in a stretcher beneath the nearer one, so that we had the hearth and the fire between us. Lauder's camp-bed went under the hole in the back wall.

There was a stable beneath, so that we had horse-beasts as well as the ordinary bugs and lice, especially myriads of jumping midges, and some kind of walking flea (I suppose it was) that did not bite, but merely strolled to and fro over one's body.

I always left my shutters open so that the first light should wake me. But this was commonly at five and there was no need to get up at that hour. My firewood was stacked ready to hand and I kept a piece of dry plank hidden to start the flame. If it was not hidden someone was certain to burn it. The others only desired a large fire with plenty of flame and smoke—a fire as easy to cook over as it would be to tow a baby's perambulator with a ten-coupled engine.

When I had made a neat clean fire with a red heart, a small bright flame, and so composed that there was always a foot or two of spare dry faggot to be urged in, with a proper proportion of good burning wood,

94

say olive and oak, and a fair immixture of bad, perhaps vine and fig, then, should I go to the spring for a pail of water or out on the balcony to throw a bone down the hill, either Cap or Lauder was sure to fling my pile on it.

When I came back it would be a mere blaze, very pleasant to look at, and making fine lights and shadows in the roof, but no good for dixies or a frying pan.

"Cookee's so mean about his wood," was the notion that supported them in this madness.

And when the fire was dying, when we had come in from a long march by way of the new batteries in Shiroska mountain, the maxims at Dramos, or from Muričan, with broken feet, dusty throats, and empty stomachs, and found the last of the embers on the hearth fading to a Tuscan red, then Cap or Lauder would fill the big tin jug (we had no kettle) and plant it down and crush the last spark out of them. These are things that count in a war, the affairs of the household—it is the same if the household consists of no more than a billycan, a bundle of sticks, and a blanket. Man is not so much a tool-using animal, whatever Carlyle may say, as a housekeeper. Even a tramp keeps house, although it is undergoing perpetual removal, and the furniture is all in his pockets.

The harder it is to keep house the more important it becomes, and the more carefully is domesticity studied, as in war time. What is the special significance of the term "Old Soldier"? It means one who is so cunning a housekeeper that he can make himself comfortable where others are at a loss. A man who always has something eatable in his haversack and drinkable in his bottle, a reserve of tobacco and matches, a warm hole to sleep in.

If it serves as a term of abuse, it is only because the majority of people are not Old Soldiers, and not good housekeepers, and find themselves overreached. But the older the veteran as a rule, the thicker his blanket, the fatter his larder, the fuller his pouch, the sharper his eye for meat, fuel, and comfort.

There was a Mexican in Bobote, who had been a rebel with Madero, then a regular when Madero was president, and a rebel again later. He was an old soldier—always in good health and good spirits, more warmed and comfortable in his well-disposed rags than many of the rest with their sound uniforms. I asked him once what he would do when the war was over, but he assured me (in case I might be troubled about his future) that there was always a war in Mexico, if the Balkans failed him, and he had no fear of being homeless or unemployed.

Whereas we were often on the edge of homelessness—when Lauder had privately wolfed all the milk, or Cap broke out and burnt up twenty hours' wood in one glorious jubilee bonfire.

The old woman who lived in a shoe had a far less improvident family than the cookee of Bobote, and not only were they improvident, but precociously unfilial. To strangers it must often have seemed that the cookee was inferior in rank to both Captain and Lieutenant—his clothes were in worse repair and his face dirtier. But it is well known that clothes do not make the man, nor Captains and Lieutenants good stew; that the pot-stick is mightier than the sword, the hearth the centre of civilization, and plain food more indispensable than high thinking.

Schedule of work for a Cookee, a Doctor, and a Dresser of Bobote

Cookee.

6.30.   Get into shirt and breeches and make fire. Roll up sack.

6.40.   Go for water—and tell the crowd outside to hold their whist and stop poking their bayonets through the wicker work—the big doctor is asleep.

7.   Put on the jug, and smoke a pipe.

7.30.   A cup of tea for each man. "Thank you Cookee," from Cap. A snore from Lauder.

8.   Ready with pan and bread for breakfast. Lift Lauder two or three inches by the hair, and wait till he opens his mouth wide enough to say, "All right, Cookee, go to hell!" Pay no attention to his eyes, though they be still shut. If he speaks intelligently to this effect he is very likely awake.

8.5 or 10 or 15.   Breakfast.

There are two kinds of breakfast, the European breakfast and the Balkan breakfast. The first is eggs and bacon fat, the second bacon fat and bread.

The first is only possible when someone has lately made the Muričan march, and found the Albanians there willing to sell their eggs. The second is more commonly used, and is a very good breakfast.

8.30. Drag Lauder from his bed, and make the bed as far as possible uninhabitable.

9.30. Smoke.

10. Make the stew and put it on.

11. Sprinkle the floor, sweep, and wash up. In sweeping it is only necessary to rub the dust gently to and fro with a besom, and it will fall through the cracks into the stable. Overhaul the stock of provisions and find out what is wanted. If beans, or rice, or bacon fat, send off one of the guards to find a mule and fetch them. If he does not return in two or three days, send another man.

12. or so to 1. or so. Smoke, feed fire, stir stew, and boil water for Lauder's dressings.

1. or so. Ladle out the lunch.

(Cap. "What's the pigwash to-day?")

(Lauder. "I wish this show was managed like the Tripoli one. They saw that we had decent food there. Ali Baba *was* a cook now"... long story about Ali Baba.)

2. Brew coffee.

2.30. Put on boots and puttees, fill a haversack, and march.

5. Remake the fire, and boil up the tea.

5.30. Make the hoosh-koosh for and put on supper. Watch dixie, and fire; grind or roast coffee (but Cap generally roasted) till 7. or 8. or so.

Ladle out supper, and give each man a piece of hard as well as a spoon of soft.

8.30 or 9. Wash up. Scour the dixies with a burnt stick, throw out any bones. Put some beans to soak in water. Light your pipe, and unroll your sack (first kicking away any stones or sticks that may cause unevennesses in the floor) and turn in.

Doctor.

7.30. Say, "Thank you Cookee," and drink tea.

7.30 to 8. Pretend to be asleep.

8.2. Spring madly out of your sack, roll it up, wrestle into coat, breeches, and boots, sit down at the fire, slap yourself on the knees, and call out, "What's for breakfast? Any eggs?" If there are eggs, take the lid of a billycan and balance it on a fork, rub it with a rasher of fat, and fry.

97

8.30.   Wash in hot water, with soap, often as far as the waist.

9.   Light a cigarette, put on your hat, and sit down to make a mousetrap.

12.–1.   Set mousetrap and go for a walk, unless in consultation with Lauder.

1.   Lunch. Look at the mousetrap for a catch.

1.15.   Drink your coffee, and then twist the cup about in a contemplative way until another brew is suggested.

2.5.   March.

5.   Tea.

5.30.   Look at mousetrap in cupboard. Smoke and roast coffee till

7.30 or 8. or so.   Supper. Look at mousetrap.

8.30.   Go to your wolsey, and read and smoke yourself to sleep, unless, as frequently,

10.30, or 11. or 12. or 1.   In comes a man with a bullet in his belly. In that case there is a getting up, a pulling on of breeches, a lighting of candles, a clearing out of bystanders, and plenty of work still to be done.

3. or 4. in the morning.   Wake for a quarter of an hour. Smoke a cigarette and look at mousetrap.

Dresser.

7.   Wake, get up stealthily, take a piece of lint and a sheet of paper or a faggot, creep cautiously about the floor, and remove any traces of the puppy's misbehaviour before Cap wakes up. Either that, or don't wake, and trust to God.

8.30.   Say, "Damn you, Cookee," when he pulls you from bed by the hair.

8.40 to 9.   Eat with gravity, gaze thoughtfully into the fire, allow the pup to chew your puttees, already the disgrace of the whole force, enquire, "Did you put any leaves into this tea, Cookee?"

9.   Get up, stretch, kick the logs, and demand your hat.

9.–9.20.   Hunt by all hands for hat, found at last in the bottom of the bed.

9.30.   Become furiously energetic, clap on hat, say, "Come on, Borjo," to the interpreter, and rush out among the patients.

10.   Appear suddenly and say, "Cookee, has the pup had any milk?" and disappear.

10.30.   Come in for hot water, and discuss technical and bloodthirsty matters with Cap.

10.35.   Out again with Cap.

11. 11.30. 12. 12.30.   The same repeated.

1.–2.   Lunch, cigarettes, coffee.

Afternoon.   March with occasional stops and howls of "Pup, pup, pup, damn that pup!"
      Carry pup home.

5.   Tea, three cups. "Don't be so mean with the milk, Cookee. Let me pour it out for myself. We may as well have it while there's any left."

5.30.   Sit over the fire with your feet in the ashes, and your head sunk into the remains of your coat collar, roll cigarettes, and tell Cookee how Ali Baba managed your meals in Tripoli.

7.30 or so.   Supper. Argue with Cookee about Home Rule.

9. or so.   Dry the plates while Cookee washes. Say, "This dishcloth is pretty scandalous, I should imagine."

10.–11.   Sit over fire and nurse puppy. Occasionally straighten the candle, or kick a log. This until Cap and Cookee are nearly asleep.

11.–12.   Chop wood with terrific pounding, scraping, panting, swearing, and pay no attention to the raging fury of Cap and Cookee, who are bounced up and down on the floor in their sacks, at every blow.

12.–1.   Take off your coat, boots, and puttees, sometimes your breeches also, scratch yourself for the time it takes to smoke two cigarettes, build up the fire, put the pup in his box, blow out the candle, and go to bed.

1.5.   Receive the pup into bed with you, and go to sleep, unless as in Cap's case (see above).

About six o'clock the maxims would begin to get very noisy, and the sharpshooters were firing at three minutes' intervals.

The guard on the forward walls of the Montenegrin outposts on Tarabos had to be changed in the dark, because the road was covered by the Turkish trenches.

This road ran along the side of the ridge through Bobote, Vallos, Dramos, and Crepaj. Crepaj was on the side of Tarabos itself, and to all

99

purposes uninhabitable. The maxims were on a spur at Dramos, and the Maxim men lived in a cottage below the spur. There was a rock above Dramos, which was used as a watch-tower, and a cave behind it for ammunition—cartridges, hand-grenades, and rockets for signalling.

Vallos was about five hundred yards in front of Bobote, and had half a battalion in it. Men were occasionally picked off there (we had one shot while playing cards, and another while putting the weight with a round stone) but it was only by chance shots.

Bobote itself stood behind a spur and the one or two shells which reached it were aimed at the ridge above, intended either for the batteries or the men bringing ammunition to them.

But the road from Vallos on was always likely to be sniped, while that from Dramos to Crepaj, and Crepaj to the first Montenegrin wall on Tarabos was not passable except in the dark. Even then there were men hit on it every night.

Crepaj was about three hundred yards from the Turks and right under their noses, so that they got many easy shots. The only disadvantage they had was that they were obliged to lean out and shew their heads against the sky in order to fire at that steep angle, while the maxims at Dramos were always waiting for them, as well as the marksmen at the walls.

The dark green kalpak of the Turkish regulars shews up bravely against the light and got many of them killed.

At bed time there was always some firing from the battery overhead, and our tiles would rattle. This firing continued generally through the night at every half hour, with again a gust or two from the maxims.

The order at the time of changing the guard was—a shell from our batteries overhead, a snap-shot or two from the Turks to shew they did not care, and a rattle from Dramos to keep their heads down, which was as much a regular order as supper itself, and provided a sort of orchestra for it.

Our coffee was good, and made in a proper way. Cap roasted it, Lauder and I ground it. It was roasted to the colour of milk chocolate, and ground fine in a brass mill. I brewed it in a small tin jug, putting plenty of coffee and sugar into pretty hot water and boiling it till the grounds sank. This is the way to make Turkish coffee. You can add a pinch of salt if you like. The grounds will float at first and make a firm crust on the water—you must leave room in the jug for the water to boil over the crust without spilling. Three boilings over will generally

precious orange put bodily
in, and set ~~stewing~~ in
a nest of embers raked
out from the logs., while
we ~~quiet~~ sat round with ~~the~~
~~sailors~~ and any chance
travellers, to watch it
and smoke, and tell
stories
at last, to our ranks.
William and I slept under
the gallery beams - enormous
rough baulks of oak curving
with their grain and only
~~lost in the~~ straight in
the one plane
§ There was a hole between
the stones that fitted my
hip, my rolled pea jacket
made a good firm pillow,
~~the two who burst shrapnel~~ shell
cases of two burst shrapnel
stood near to promise me

The Only Extant Page from Cary's Draft Manuscript

make the grounds sink. If they don't, go on with it. You do not need a strainer or any fallals, the coffee will be clear.

I lay under the window between the hearth and the wall. The wall was wicker-work, and the guard slept on the other side of it, with a plank laid on the rafters of the gallery for a bed. I could just see the outline of his shoulder when I lay on my left side; when I lay on my right I watched the fire, and the smoke drifting up to the high beams of the roof.

We had a bayonet for candlestick, stuck point down in a crack of the hearth, with the candle in its socket. Lauder blew it out before he went to his blankets.

28

The mousetraps were engines built in the great style, on Roman lines, of two inch boards weighted with ten pound stones. They would have held a badger, and killed mice in a thoroughly humane manner. Cap used the embrasure of a window for workshop and was so absorbed in the work (humming or whistling to himself, generally in his shirt but always wearing his hat) that I treated him as a fixture when sweeping out, like the hearthstone, and sprinkled round him.

If Cap was in before lunch he would take off his coat and draw Tigers and Hippopotamuses on the walls with the point of the bayonet. The walls were well smoked and made an excellent ground. By the end of April they were decorated in a way that must have greatly improved the value and interest of the house.

29

Lauder's puppy was a yellow bitch about the size of a fox terrier. He brought her into our household on the grounds of altruistic humanity, but really because he liked her.

He had often told us of the great loot he had taken after the February battle in Obote, a village down by the river: mats, pottery, carved work and left at Oblique in the care of Mam'selle.

He pointed out how useful the mats would be every time a fork, plate, or slice of toast fell through our floor, and at last took a whole day's leave to go to Oblique for them.

When he came back in the evening Cap and I were sitting over the fire, Cap turning the coffee roaster, I grinding, and sucking at a pipe.

Lauder had a yellow parcel under his arm. He advanced and put it down on the hearthstone between us, under the candle.

"Isn't she a lovely dear," he said. The lovely dear stood, sneezed, and gravely misbehaved herself upon the ashes.

We both started up in great indignation and aimed our feet at her. Lauder caught her up in his arms and lectured us.

He told us he had found her starving in an empty village. Her brother was with her, but the brother had a less dainty appetite and was under suspicion of body snatching; of living on Stevenson's strange meats.

We adopted her into the force because plainly she could not be turned out.

It is a delicate subject, but it is understood that the puppy had been very badly brought up. We could not put her out at night because she howled, and apart from the danger of some one of a hundred wakened soldiers putting his bayonet into her, Lauder suffered like a mother. His head came out from the blankets at the first snicker, one watched him wait painfully, and then the howl went through him like a bullet. She had to be allowed to stay in therefore. She shewed the only touch of humane affection we could find in her by respecting Lauder's blankets, but Cap and I both slept on the floor defenceless.

The first morning that Cap made a discovery, he said so many hard things that Lauder was really grieved for the puppy and afraid she should be turned out again. I therefore said nothing of my own finds. But it was a few days after this that I was waked about four o'clock by a louder gunshot than usual (the same gun will often make a double noise—it depends on the wind) and heard someone move in the room. Cap's end was of course all dark, mine in a pale twilight. Suddenly a naked figure appeared on tiptoe from Cap's end, stopped to yawn outrageously and then proceeded to quarter the floor in a crouching attitude. This was the Lauder that had to be dragged from bed most mornings by the hair. The pup strolled after him with a sleepy gape, turning at each corner.

30

We were not long in Bobote when Gospodin Michan Plomenatz came to see us.

He rode up one evening on his white pony and burst upon us in a bustle. He brought his maid with him. Gospodin Michan told us he had come this time only to amuse himself.

The Plomenatz indeed had advanced very much in power during the war. They were suspects in the beginning, but by this time, Colonel Plomenatz, a cousin of Mike's, who had started as an officer of commissariat at the base, was chief of staff at Muričan and a great man. He deserved all his greatness. The Colonel was one of the most capable men they had—hard working, level-headed, good-tempered. Gospodin Michan was proud of him and would not now interpret for anyone inferior in rank to Cap.

The bringing of the maid puzzled us. The journey had been heavy for her, she had hard lying even in the stretcher I lent her for a bed (Lauder gave Mike his bed), the food was bad, she was shy and kept herself in a corner, and she did not work.

She was indeed rather astonished when I gave her the besom the next day, and made her sweep.

Todd came over the mountain that morning with a sack of potatoes and onions for us, begged from the Sergeant-Major.

He was greatly intrigued by the presence of Storka, and I saw Lauder in deep confidence with him upon matters which I could not but suspect were scandal, by the look of his eye, the set of his neck, and the bristle of his beard.

I had a sore foot at this time, which sometimes kept me in. The others went up the mountain, and the maid went with them. They took Todd as far as the battery on the ridge on his way back to Zogaj, saw the afternoon's firing, and came down.

Lauder and Cap both regarded me as I sat innocently smoking over the hearth with a stick in my hand and an eye on the dixie, in a manner of suppressed delight which pointed to revelations and chaff. These looks continued all the evening. Cap even burst into chuckles and kicked the logs at intervals. Mike was graver than usual, and Storka helped me to wash up with an air of nervous confusion which decided me in my notion that she was an ass.

"I say, Cookee," said Lauder, when the two of us were alone after lunch on the day after (Mike and the maid were down the gully looking for the horse) "are you well fixed in England?" He then laughed loudly.

"What do you mean?"

"You don't own a sixpenny-good-pull-for-carmen by any chance?"
"No!"

"Then it's no good, Cookee," said Lauder, and explained that Mike had been sounding them about my position in life, character, and prospects.

"You were to marry Storka, and take up some of Mike's land," said Lauder.

Storka and Mike came in at that moment and I looked critically at my proposed wife. She smiled at me, and wiped her pretty nose on her hand with an embarrassed air. Gospodin Michan sat down and poked the logs with the coffee roaster, and cursed his horse by the name of son-of-a-bitch of a damn-horse.

He took occasion a little later to say that it was a son-of-a-bitch country anyhow and that he thought he would go back to America as soon as he could get some likely young feller to take up his farm. I tried to look as likely as possible, and asked several agricultural questions.

But the romance was all destroyed some time that same day. Mike found out from either Cap or Lauder that I was not inclined to settle in the Black Mountain, that as a rule I was a man of no occupation, not at all well fixed, and gave up his match-making.

He left for Virpazar the next day by way of Zogaj and a boat, and took Storka with him.

I do not know now that it would not be a good life to live in a Black Mountain farm with Storka. She was a good girl and a handsome girl, of the most grave presence; there is no reason why everyone should not blow his or her nose as he or she thinks fit, and a Montenegrin wife would be a wife of spirit, character, and courage, with a mind of her own, and a most upstanding family.

31

A squad of recruits turned up this week from Mexico and were remarkable in the camp for their terrific warrior-like air, outsoldiering the toughest of the veterans. It was probably not so much a pose, as their customary swagger of peace contrasted violently with the easy and gentle appearance of the real fighting men. In the same way young men are judged poseurs when they first come to a University.

The moralist says Ha! Ha! they are already thinking themselves grown up—look at the poor hobbledehoyish struts of them. Actually what is seen is the end of an old manner, not the beginning of a new. Freshmen are public-school bloods fresh from big-side Levee, and full of manly importance greater than that of a general of seventy. The good are graver and more proper than bishops, and the bad worse than Panurge. The second-year are lambs and sucking-doves compared to them. It is with shy embarrassment that a Don asks them to breakfast, or the Captain of the Boats invites them to the barge, and tells them that ponchos will be allowed if they find themselves too tender in the behind for childish sports.

Blues make way for them in the High, and the Proctor trembles as he accosts them after dark to ask for their name and college. In the same way did our flag-men timidly avoid these recruits, and smooth their voices when they sent them to duty.

32

About the 20th of March Cap and Todd went to Antivari for mails, Lauder, I, and the pup were left in charge.

There was little doing in the batteries and trenches beyond the ordinary routine firing of the day, and a skirmish between the outposts each evening when the guard was changed.

The walls were carried forward a yard or two each night, and one or two wounded came in.

Cap and Todd had the last eggs for their marching-breakfast, and we went to Muričan that afternoon for more.

It was a hot day like most of our days. We dropped down across the stony hillside below Bobote to the wooded downs of the valley, broke through a thicket to river level, and bathed in the last pool of Muričan brook. Then climbed laboriously up Muričan to the old gun-positions and sat down to wait for the pup—and smoke.

From Muričan we could see the whole line of the ridge—one tree-pass, the old Turkish sangars (that were still full of dead) above Vilgar, Shiroska Mountain and the guns perched on it like crows, the Nipple where a maxim was, the Navel, Big Tarabos with its forts and trenches and crown of wire, and the zig-zag walls of the Montenegrin pioneers on its flank, the plateau with the Turkish guns in a row, and Little Tarabos by the river. We ate our bread and onions over this con-

... *we could see the whole line of the ridge—*

templation, and then turned down to Murican village—five or six ruined cottages, a farm house for the General Martinović, his staff, and the field post office.

There were two girls selling wine, raki, and coffee, each with a ring of soldiers squatted about her fire. Half a dozen Albanians made a group by themselves under a tree in their white breeches and white fezzes, gravely smoking, and never saying a word. We bought a bottle of wine, ordered coffee, saw it ground and set to brew in a tin among the embers, and looked about for acquaintances.

Gospodin Michan's brother was there and saluted us in the proper manner—one salute, a handshake and a bow, then another salute and an invitation to drink. He was a portly old gentleman, and the immense long barrelled revolver, which all Montenegrins carry in the front of their sash, stood at a long distance from his backbone.

But he was very polite and perfectly hospitable. He had no news for us, except that it was proposed to move the Oblique guns to a hill nearer the river, and that eight new howitzers were promised from Russia with a thousand rounds apiece.

We met the Prince Mirko also, riding from Oblique way to see Martinović. There are three princes, Danilo, a stolid-looking fellow, Mirko with a flash air, and Peter Peter, I never met, but he is the most popular. Mirko hollowed his back very much when he saluted, and stooped to give us three flabby fingers, bending from the thigh, like Punch when he beats Judy. Possibly we were too dirty for his dignity when his own guardsmen were watching. He confirmed the arrival of the new guns, said there was likely to be an attack soon, asked after Cap, repeated the salute and handshakes, and rode by. We went off to get the eggs.

You object again that this history is all of meals, of stew and eggs.

Anyone will tell you that a war is not made up of fighting, but just exactly of stew, and if you are lucky, eggs. Just as the life of an American woman does not consist altogether of marriages and divorces, with homicide here and there, but of stew and eggs, and such matters.

Lauder and I marched up to the first farm. There were three at Murican. The farmers were Albanian refugees escaped from Scutari.

At the first farm this was the conversation (I spell phonetically). The farmer stood on his gallery, we below.

LAUDER: Dobra vetcha, gospodin. (Good evening)

FARMER: Dobra ve stretcha. (Good luck to you sir)

I: Imma ya-ya? (There are eggs?)

FARMER, spreading out his hands palm up: Nema netcha gospodin. (Not none at all)

LAUDER: Damned old scoundrel. Come along Cookee.

At the second farm we knew there was a better chance. An exactly similar conversation did not cause Lauder to say "damned old scoundrel." He walked up the steps and repeated: "Imma ya-ya, imma mnogo, snahm." (There are eggs, plenty of eggs, I know) "Kolika para?" I added (How many pence?) to show we meant to pay.

The farmer led us into his cottage. It was clean, though not so clean as the farmer and the farmer's wife, whose white clothes were spotless. The baby was clean too, but almost choked by a stout blanket put over his cradle, like most of their babies.

We sat down on a mat beside the fire, and the farmer, squatting before us, made us cigarettes.

The woman of the house meanwhile brewed us coffee and milk, a great delicacy, the coffee boiled in the milk with plenty of sugar. No one referred to eggs until we had swallowed the coffee and smoked the cigarettes, with several ejaculations of "Dobra cafa, fala mnogo, gospodja." (Good coffee, thank you very much, madam). I do not think this was etiquette. Our thanks should have been addressed to the man, and pretty madam looked very shy for the whole session.

When we had refused a second cup of coffee, the farmer brought out his eggs, and we purchased them all, twenty at rather less than a penny each.

The march back was like all the marches back, very heavy going, with Bobote steadily rising in our thoughts until it seemed the very centre of comfortable civilization, fire, tea, light, and bed.

33

The day after Muričan we went to Oblique to see the famous Mam'selle, and the gun positions.

Oblique is some six miles from Bobote. It faces Little Tarabos, and its batteries were directed towards the Turkish guns on the plateau. To a certain extent they also covered the river.

Lauder saw all his patients by twelve, we filled our haversacks with bread, bully, and chocolate, our waterbottles with cold coffee, and marched off.

The road for the first part of the way is the outpost road through Vilgar, Bobote, Vallos, and Dramos, where the maxims were. All this road is covered by the Turkish snipers on Tarabos, but they rarely hit anybody until they had passed Dramos.

We had several wounded in from Vallos, two thousand metres from Tarabos, but the shots were very lucky. At Dramos we turned down behind a bluff. The river runs down a deep gully beyond this bluff, and its banks give cover for most of the way. It was exciting getting over the bluff, because it is a perfectly smooth face of pale brown stone reflecting the light, and making even our khaki look black, a very good mark for the Turks at seven hundred. But once in the river-bed, picking one's way from stone to stone, Tarabos was hidden for most of the time, and the run of the water, shallows and pools, the bushes, the little capes and bays, made it a fine country for travelling.

We knew the house at Oblique by the tricolor flying from the windows. The puppy's brother came out to meet his sister, a sight which caused Lauder a great deal of pleasure. Mam'selle followed. She was a tall sallow woman, good looking and strong, dressed in the Albanian way, white blouse and sash, loose white trousers, white slippers. Monsieur was a little man with a brown virgin beard, very fair complexion, blue protruding eyes, smoking a large briar pipe of which he was plainly very proud. Mam'selle had been with the advance-guard of the army from the first. She was a capable nurse, hard-working, courageous. Monsieur, and Doctor Beyer of the Swiss Red Cross, who was with Vukotić, were the only two doctors besides the English doctors who did any field work in Montenegro.

We were received very warmly at Oblique, and had a good lunch. Mam'selle argued at times with M'sieu, looking at him with her eye-lids half dropped in a most dramatic manner, while M'sieu's eyes opened so widely that they seemed ready to pop out of his head.

We were sometimes appealed to, but gave Delphian replies, which were claimed by each side as a favourable judgment.

But M'sieu was a delightful fellow, candid, brave, energetic. He had a pompous little manner, a quick, petulant, foot-tapping, eye-popping sort of way which was exceedingly comic, but not at all to be laughed at. He chewed his immense bulldog pipe with a determination to be "sportif," that could not be taken but with seriousness. We discussed English tobaccos with him. I gave him a fill of hardcut, which he said was "un peu fort, but of a fine bouquet."

In the afternoon we went with them to see the new gun positions. M'sieu skipped along in front, turning at every fourth stone to pull out his pipe and ejaculate a remark. Mam'selle wished to take us out of our way to see some *belles cadavres* (beautiful corpses) which desire M'sieu considered to be a piece of mere femininity not to be given way to. So that we were always enlivened by an argument which threatened at any moment to drag us into indiscretion. Two people of character cannot live long together without affording each other plenty of ammunition for a fight.

We found one big gun already in its emplacement—a fifteen centimetre howitzer. The gunners told us that it could be used against the Turkish guns on the plateau in the next assault. When was the next assault to be? Soon, they told us.

Oblique was shelled just after our return from the hill. It was not so God-forsaken a wild place as Zogaj or Vilgar or Bobote—there were fields and downs round it, with sheep grazing, and the bursting of shells seemed almost as incongruous as it would be in a quiet village of Louth or Kildare.

M'sieu kept us eating and drinking all day and would not let us go till dark. Then we had to wait for a moon.

The moon was nearly at full. We started out from a last cup of wine, and the hearty invitation to stay of Mam'selle and M'sieu, sure of our way; but soon lost it.

To be lost in those wildernesses of little hills and deep gullies, with the chance of blundering into a dangerous corner, is bad for the temper. Lauder cursed Cookee, and I cursed Lauder and the pup.

A skirmish broke out luckily on the slopes of Tarabos, and the maxims at Dramos began to be noisy. We guided ourselves by this and climbed straight across hedge, stream, thicket, bog, and rock, till we reached Dramos. There were many bullets flying down the road as we came along, and we found four wounded just brought in when we arrived.

I lit a fire and boiled the water; Lauder, who could barely stand for fatigue, cleared the other room of the soldiers, spread sheepskins for his patients, and made his examination. Two were hit in the legs, one thigh, one calf, no harm done, one in the forearm, but no more than a chip out of the flesh—the fourth was shot through the belly.

The best thing that can happen for a man hit in the belly is to be forgotten. Let him alone, don't shake him, and his gut will close up quickly. This man had been carried from Dramos, up and down three miles of stony hillsides, and was lucky if he escaped peritonitis.

We kept him three days on milk, and he was better. Then his friends stole him, and we never saw him again.

34

Captain Marcović was a slim, tall young fellow with long moustaches, always in a very smart uniform, as befitted his position on Martinović's staff.

He had a misfortune in this month which would not have been a misfortune anywhere else but in Montenegro. He was sent into Scutari with another officer on a parley. They went to warn Essad that the civil population should be sent out of the town before another assault. Essad refused, and the two officers set out to return, walking their horses over the first rough ground.

The Turks began immediately to fire at them. The two were right in the open, at short range. The first of them jumped on his horse to get away. Marcović's horse was restive, frightened by the firing, and could not be mounted without a struggle, which in some way or another broke the sling of the Captain's sword. The sword was lost, and Marcović (wearing a big cloak over his uniform) did not know it till he got back to cover.

According to the fixed tradition one must not lose one's sword under any circumstances. Marcović had the choice of going back for it and most certainly being shot, or facing the scandal.

He chose to be killed, but in a more useful way. He undertook to take command in the next assault on Tarabos.

He came into Bobote on the 30th of March to tell us the situation.

It must be explained that on Tarabos trench digging was nearly impossible. The whole ridge is either hard rock or broken rocks with a little stony earth between.

The Turkish fort on the top was blasted out some time ago, their other trenches with the exception of a redoubt just inside the second line of wire, where there were excellent bomb proofs, were shallow. The chief defence was the wire.

The Montenegrins were attacking now the second line of wire (they forced the third in February) and the redoubt.

They had built a zig-zag wall up the side of the mountain to the wire.

It was the most interesting thing in the world to watch the progress of this wall from day to day. The building was all done by a special corps of 120 pioneers working in twelve-hour shifts. A stone was pushed out at the end of the wall, another put upon it, and so on. Meanwhile they were so close to the Turks during the last weeks that even a hand could be seen by the sharp-shooters—we had many of the pioneers shot through the palm in this very process of pushing out a stone. [See Notes, figure on p. 154.]

When the wall was near the wire the Turks ran a counter wall down from the Redoubt inside the wire, to enfilade it. The pioneers then put a T. piece on the end of their wall while the guns on Shiroska Gora knocked the Turks out of theirs.

The T. piece brought the attackers to the wire. They blew it up with hand-grenades and cut it with pliers, all but the top wire, which was too high. It must be said that grenades and shell are very little good against wire.

In this case the entanglement was four posts wide, about ten feet. The wire was $\frac{1}{8}$ inch thick, the barbs $\frac{1}{2}$ inch long and a half-inch apart. These barbs were loose, merely twisted round the wire.

The posts were five feet high as a rule, but varied according to their depth in the ground.

The wire was crossed and recrossed from post to post, back and forwards, as well as carried straight, so that there was no getting through it even if no one was shooting at you from fifteen yards range.

A shell merely throws up all this wire and tangles it more than ever. A shot that levels one post will not affect the others unless they are in line. Of course they must not be in line.

That is, there is still left a triple wire as well as the remains of the first, still formidable, even if a shot should break a post. The hand grenade is less effective, it will not even break the post.

All this entanglement had been battered for months. The ground was torn to pieces—the posts at all angles—but it was just as difficult an entanglement as ever.

The only way with wire is to sap up to it and cut it.

If you have some thousands of men to lose for very little progress, you can storm it. Take up coats and blankets and planks to throw over it and let the bodies of the first two lines make a bridge over it for the third.

The Servians tried to storm the wire at Brditza in February. Some of them got inside it and were shot there. Some of them were bayoneted by a counter charge as they stuck on the barbs.

The Turks then murdered the wounded at their leisure. And this was the outer wire of Brditza covering a great length of ground and thinly defended. At each successive wire in an attack on such mountain positions as Tarabos and Brditza the defence is more concentrated as the defenders are driven in.

About five yards of wire were cut at the end of the Montenegrin wall by the last day of March. The redoubt was twenty yards up from this gap. There were also side trenches from the redoubt in each direction round the hillside, at the same distance from the wire.

The attack was to be led, so Marcović told us, by Colonel Plomenatz with a mixed battalion—ten volunteers from each of the others and Marcović second in command.

The Cettinski battalion under Captain Martinović was in the second line. The Komerskozagaratchski battalion on the Navel, and the Chefskobielitski (I think) in reserve for the Cettinski.

The Lechanski were on the other side of Tarabos towards the lake. It was hoped to blow a second gap in the wire for the Komerskozagaratchski and the latter battalion during the battle, to let them get at the side trenches and prevent a flanking movement by the Turks, should the redoubt be taken.

Three maxim parties were to go with the mixed battalion.

The Montenegrins relied very much on rapidity of fire. On the whole I should think the shooting of both sides was bad and that Turks and Montenegrins relied both on quantity. I judge only by the amount of bullets flying even in the skirmishes where there could have been nothing to shoot at.

The Cettinski and Komerskozagaratchski battalions both lived in Bobote, so that a great many of our friends were fighting. Marcović we knew, Martinović we knew, and the Colonel was a friend of Cap's.

The evening was passed in discussion of the place we should take in the battle.

Crepaj was too near and the wounded would get killed. In the case of defeat they would all get killed. It was only three hundred yards from the Turks and right under their rifles. They could drop stones into it.

To choose Dramos, on the other hand, meant that the wounded would have to cross the most dangerous piece of open ground in the whole field—that between Dramos and Crepaj—there were at least a few trees at Crepaj. There was also a ruined cottage there, with enough roof to keep out shrapnel, or make it ineffective.

The Montenegrins, of course, had no medical corps of their own at all, no stretchers, no bearers. It was therefore important for us to be as far up as possible.

We chose Crepaj and decided to get there in the dark, the night before the battle, that is, on the night of April 1st.

The next day Cap made a last journey to Zogaj to tell them to expect a batch of wounded, while Lauder and I finished the packing of stores.

In the afternoon Lauder went to the Brigadier at Vilgar mosque for carriers. He had prepared for this negotiation in his customary manner —by walking three or four times round the room, cutting a tag or two off his puttees, buttoning two buttons of his coat, tilting his hat over his eyes, and scrubbing his beard with his hands—then walked off in silent meditation. He returned however in two minutes to say:

"How many men do you want, Cookee?"

"Eight."

"Come on, pup, pup, pup. Damn that pup!"

The Brigadier sent eight men of the relief that evening, and we dispatched all our stores to Crepaj.

I give a list:

700 roller bandages
Wool to match
Double cyanide gauze
Two pound bottles of iodine
Lysol
Field haversack, with scissors, boracic etc.
Two dressing bowls
About a hundred first field dressings, all we had
Two lanterns
One tin jug
Two billycans

Twelve loaves of bread
Two dozen candles
A bag of rice
A bag of beans
Four tins of bully
Twelve tins of milk
½ lb. of tea
A kilo of sugar
Three cups

The emergency rations, two a man, were packed in the haversacks. Cap and Lauder of course had their own instrument cases.

35

We had arranged to go with the outpost at six as far as Dramos rock, and take advantage of the dark to reach Crepaj that night.

But when it was time, we decided to have a good night's sleep instead, and march in the morning when the battle should begin.

We spent the evening coffee-roasting and arguing with Borjo, who was not convinced that Crepaj was the best place to go to.

Borjo was a fat, large, shiny-faced man with a black beard. He had kept a restaurant in San Francisco. He was therefore particular never to help in our cooking, for although Equality and Fraternity were ever in his mouth, he was a snob.

Lauder and I were so indignant at his opposition to Crepaj, that we called him a bum, but I think that was too strong. A bum is after all a very low sort of fellow, while Borjo was only mediocre. Borjo had plenty of courage of course, but so have all the Montenegrins—even those Yankees who were accustomed to say good-bye in an affecting manner every time they went for a walk, and suggest that they would certainly be killed before long. They contradicted prejudice, and fought as well as anybody else.

When in the morning at seven I went for water to make the tea, the village was already empty. Usually there were twenty or thirty at the water washing their faces and gossiping, with four or five women rinsing clothes—my bucket often went up a line of ten hands to the

First Advance on Tarabos (opposite page)

spring. I picked my way over the stones that morning with a feeling of Sunday.

The day was clear, and the hillsides all manner of colours, but broadly divided into silver and blue—the sky pale with diffused sunlight, and no wind about.

There were very few shots to be heard, not one in five minutes—the usual five-minute snap-shot from the sniper at the right hand loophole in Tarabos main fort.

We had the European breakfast at eight, and walked out at a quarter to nine. The sniping had stopped altogether and there was dead silence. First marched Cap, twirling a walking-stick, then Lauder, then Borjo, then I. It was growing very hot and we took off our coats before we came up to Vallos. Vallos was deserted save for one old man, wounded some days before in the leg, who sat smoking an inordinately long pipe (a hot coal balanced on the bowl) under the eaves of the mosque.

As we left Vallos the first gun sounded from Shiroska hill. Cap pulled out his watch. It was exactly the hour given by Marcović, nine o'clock. Eight shells were fired in the first minute—and broke the quiet of the morning with their screaming and sobbing, as they went over us on their way down the ridge. We saw the earth fly out of the top of Tarabos.

In ten minutes the Turks began to reply with common shell, which burst on the face of Shiroska. We had agreed to watch the bombardment from the rock over Dramos, at eight hundred yards from the Turkish redoubts, and arrived there before ten. We had comfortable places, with plenty of cover and an excellent outlook over the positions.

There was little rifle fire—and I heard very few bullets, the bombardment was too hot. We saw one man go up bodily in the dust of a melinite shell, spread-eagled.

The Montenegrins did not advance to the forward wall or they would have been hit by their own guns. One shell went astray as it was and killed the Commandant of the Komerskozagaratchski and a priest, who had gone too far along the crest.

At two o'clock the fire was shifted higher and changed to shrapnel, which shewed us that the attack was going to begin. The shrapnel was to keep the Turks' heads down.

The front wall, the T. piece at the end of the last zig-zag, began to fill. We could see the sheepskin coats of the men as they squatted behind it.

At the same time bullets began to strike our rock and more passed overhead. Borjo's cap was touched and moved an inch or two across his skull. Cap damned us both and told us to keep our heads down. A line of men appeared suddenly on the sky line from the far side of the ridge, silhouetted, and ran stumbling towards the wire.

These were the bomb-throwers. There were forty of them, all old men and special volunteers. They offered themselves because as they said it would not matter if they got killed. Several of them were wearing the long white frock, blue breeches and white stockings of civil dress, and their coats blew out ludicrously behind them as they hurried their rheumatic old legs over the stones.

The bombs were tubes about eight feet long, meant to be pushed under the wire and fired by a fuse. They proved more effective than either shells or grenades, though not so good as pliers.

Several of the old men went down, but two thirds of them got their bombs into position and lighted. They came trotting back with short steps and long jumps as men do over rough ground, falling one by one all the time. When they passed immediately above the walls and the soldiers waiting there, they threw up their caps to shew them that the wire was broken.

It must be understood that the Turks were firing point blank at them from fifty yards. Some of those who threw their caps too high waited gravely for them to come down again, as if it was a game of cup and ball.

About half these men were killed outright, all but two or three were hit, some had five, one seven holes in him.

The gunners aimed now at the very summit, and even clean over to catch the Turkish supports coming along the road from Little Tarabos.

The Servians meanwhile fired shrapnel in salvoes at Brditza, on the other side of the Bojana. The shells were perfectly timed, and at each discharge the head of the mountain was surrounded by a ring of bursting shells as neat as a wreath of roses. This fire was intended to keep the Turks at Brditza from sending help to Tarabos by way of the bridges, although the Servians actually had no intention of attacking.

Our second line, of the Cettinski Battalion, now lined out across the lower slope of Tarabos and began to climb at a leisurely pace. They were not greatly exposed. The line and the distances were perfectly kept. Their khaki and sheepskins were a little darker than the grey of the mountain side, and the whole advance was very clearly seen. The sun flashed on a sword now and then, but the triangular bayonet does not catch the light.

The gun-fire wavered, and then suddenly increased. The Turkish fort was covered with flying dirt, smoke, and pieces of sand-bag.

The first man at the end of the front Montenegrin wall stood up and walked out. He was shot in that instant, but the second, third, fourth, fifth followed in single file at distances of a yard or two, stooped under the wire and clambered towards the redoubt.

There was a little dip in the ground just beyond the wire, to the left of the gap, which gave partial cover; a party collected there and rushed up in a mass.

The Turkish rifle fire was now very fast, like the noise of a thousand summer days in one overhead, and chips flying off our rock right and left, although it was considerably dispersed by the time it reached us.

We saw Colonel Plomenatz against the sky on the top of the scarp, waving his sword. He seemed to hang for a moment, and then disappeared with a crowd of his men.

The redoubt was taken. New cover was thrown up inside the wire and the supports poured into the position. We could hear maxims going in the trenches near the redoubt.

The Turks filed quickly into the upper fort. Their heads shewed against the sky, easily seen as they moved to their places. Through Cap's glasses we watched their rifles thrust out over the sand-bags, fired, cocked up to be refilled, and dropped again.

At every half-minute a shell burst on the parapet and knocked half a dozen of them down—but supports never ceased to move in from the left. We learnt afterwards that all the Turkish trenches were evacuated during the morning's bombardment, save for the men in the bomb proofs of the lower redoubt, and a few here and there to look to the field telephones.

Plomenatz was dead. When he seemed to jump down that time, he was shot through the skull, and for ten minutes or so his battalion was in confusion. They rushed blindly up the trenches from the redoubt and were caught. The Turks had maxims facing straight down these trenches and shot them down in dozens.

In such a rabbit warren as the top of Tarabos, it is not astonishing that Marcović had some trouble in making his orders known and keeping his men together. They ran off in small parties exploring and were cut off—they walked in on maxims. There was a place beyond the redoubt called the yard, because it lay between two cross-walls, a simple enough place to blunder into as a short cut to the side trench. Nobody came out of the yard unmurdered.

At half past three we saw the first wounded straggling down the hill through the open lines of the supports.

We made a meal, waited for a burst of firing from our gunners to knock down the sharp-shooters, and went out towards Crepaj.

I noticed the spring leaves falling off the trees and it took a moment's reflection to perceive that the bullets were cutting them down.

We might have run—but it is not etiquette to run, and very little good.

Cap led the way, stick in hand, then Lauder, I, and Borjo.

Crepaj is full of low walls, and brushwood. The walls gave little cover at that angle of fire, about sixty degrees, but there were already many wounded crouched here and there under them, and lying in the bushes.

Lauder and I stopped on the way to dress an old man, one of the bomb-throwers—his right arm was shot to pieces. I suppose he was seventy years old, bent in the shanks, shaky about the chin, his long white frieze coat (a clean one for the occasion) dabbled with blood, but he was perfectly collected, and boasted that he had put his bomb in position and lighted it before he was hit.

When we went on to the cottage, we found Cap driving a crowd of wounded under cover. The house was just above the copses of the lower slope—on the bare side of Tarabos itself. It was partly ruined, but the roof was stout enough to break the force of shrapnel, there was a big stable below, walled in, a yard in front, and a loft for the stores. The loft was approached by a steep ladder. There were two broad straw beds in it and a hearth. All the rest of the floor on this storey was gone, and the little passage ended abruptly on the edge of the stable wall. There was already a small fire lit below in the middle of the stable and twenty or so wounded men lying round it.

I carried up the stores and sorted them—then went out for sticks; as stooping I pushed to and fro in the bushes, I came upon several wounded, and sent them up to the house. They were unaccustomed to find doctors about in a battle, and had been choosing quiet places to lie in, according to their habit, until either they died, or the fighting stopped and their friends came to take them away.

The front wall of the cottage was down and the roof-timbers stood on the remains of the end walls, which sheltered the two doctors from the sharp-shooters and enabled them to work in the open air. The sharp-shooters had already found us, and Borjo, seeing me approach with a bundle of faggots, waved me to keep away from that corner. But that corner was the only way of approach from the hill and many of the wounded were hit again just as they reached safety. The spring too was in the open about thirty yards beyond this place, and water carrying was touch-and-go work. The rill ran very slowly, and the water in a small hollow rock which was meant for a reservoir was full of blood from the men drinking as they came past. One took out a kerosene tin, and there was never a tin that seemed to take more filling, while one squatted on one's haunches and looked up the mountain side. It is impossible to tell whether a bullet that strikes the ground near is only a stray shot, or the first from the magazine of a sharp-shooter. Borjo and I took turns at this duty. No one was allowed to wash, but as much as could be got was hardly enough for dressings and drinking.

The Turkish gunners found our range about eight, when it was already almost dark.

Todd and Starkie, who watched the fight with the General Staff on the top of Shiroska, saw the officer who directed the fire. The guns themselves were behind Tarabos, and shot over it. This officer strolled out on the summit of the hill, looked round him at the lower slopes, and shouted directions into the fort behind. He was killed by a shell from Shiroska before he could return.

The first Turkish shrapnel burst over us in another few minutes, and the fire was continued from that until midday of the 3rd.

The shots were for the most part too short or too far, but they closed the road. Not a wounded man could stir a foot from us. At three o'clock when Cap went to the loft for two hours sleep and I took up the dressing with Lauder, they were piled up in the inner stable three and four deep, a row sitting up against the wall, a second overlapping them to the breast, a third across their legs. They looked like a congregation of fasting friars with their brown skull caps and hollow cheeks; the small fire in the middle for light, and the bare walls behind.

Many were dead, but others were asleep, we had no time to sort them out. There was an arched doorway between this inner room and our corner, which was always in a bustle. There were two lanterns slung up, two sacks of dressings lying open beneath, two bowls of lysol and warm water, a bottle of iodine in a niche. The wounded lay or stood in a close crowd about and we did not stop from washing, painting, bandaging at all. Outside the maxims never ceased, one took up the refrain from another, there was the report of big guns every minute, and now or then the crash of shrapnel like a thunder clap over the roof, but inside the house was as quiet as a church.

Some of the dying breathed hard, one or two of those waiting to be dressed talked in low voices. The priest of the mixed battalion with his cross thrust into his sash, his rifle in the crook of his arm, his long hair matted in the blood of the floor, lay at the bottom of the ladder, and opened his mouth from time to time as if he was strangling—then sighed easily and softly. Borjo, coming quickly down the ladder and trying to avoid the bayonets of the rifles which were stacked against the rungs, stepped upon him, but he made no sign of consciousness. The wounded sometimes came in excited, they had just run the gauntlet of the corner—they brought accounts of some new advance or retreat, but in a moment or so they became as impassive as the rest, squatted down if there was room, or leant on their rifles and waited their turn. Some were carried in, but if their comrades stayed to watch, they kept silence.

When at four in the morning Borjo had a sudden loud quarrel with a grenadier, whose unexploded grenade was swinging by the handle from his sash and causing indignation to some of the others, we were startled as if by an impropriety—Lauder, a picture of methodical toil all night, stood up to look, the soldiers turned round. The man was thrown out with unanimous curses to find cover in the garden (he was not wounded), Borjo returned grumbling to his work, Lauder stooped down with his probe, the soldiers fell again into listless attitudes and watched the dressing.

At dawn there was a lull in the firing; I waited for a shell to burst and then went to the spring to wash. We were all in blood to the shoulders. Two soldiers followed to drink. One of them was a Yankee, and we sat talking while he poured capfuls of water over my arms and hands.

"How you like dis country—pretty pore country, I guess."

"I like it."

"No money—son-of-a-bitch pore country. I bin in Amurka four years. Amurka's the greates' fines' country in the world—you come from Amurka, sir?"

"No, England."

"Dat's same thing, sure," he broke off suddenly as a bullet hit the stones, to glance up the hill, and ejaculated;

"Son-of-a-bitch Turski!"

"Were you in the mines in America?" I asked.

"You bet you—for two years. Then I started business in San Francisco."

"An hotel?" which is a safe question to ask of a Yankee Montenegrin that talks of his business.

"Sure—a restaurant." He described the restaurant, and the cunning with which restaurants need to be managed. How one can be trusted to pay another day, another can't.

He was especially angry at the recollection of a cousin of his own that had cheated him, and two Dagos. The two Dagos were lumped into the crowd of all Dagos as sons-of-bitches. He warned me against Eyetalian Dagos as the worst of the whole family.

Another shot overhead followed by a sudden outbreak of maxims, and a volley which knocked up the dust all round, sent us back to shelter. He made for the walls lower down the hill, but as we separated, he had the last word with "Son-of-bitches Dago Turski" which is as far as man can go in indignation.

At five Cap came down and sent me off with orders to sleep.

I pushed through the crowd over a row of outstretched legs, stepped across the body of the priest to the ladder, and climbed, feeling that it would be easy to sleep. But the firing increased with the light and more wounded came in. I made strong tea to keep myself awake and went to chop up the floor and the wicker-work wall of the back loft for dry sticks.

I had come back with the first bundle, stacked them beside the hearth, and was lighting a pipe by the window with my eye on Cap and Lauder working below, when there was an unusually fierce volley aimed at us. Cap, who stood at the outer edge of the wall, turned sharp round to see that everyone was under cover. There were three crossing those five yards at the moment, and the first and second stepped safely past under the wall. The third was an old man, wounded in the leg. He was within a yard of the wall, when a single last shot sounded overhead—he made a noise like a small dog whose tail has been trampled on, twisted half round, and fell like a sack. His cloak bellied out with the wind, fluttered and settled down upon him. He was dragged under the wall, but died in a couple of minutes. At that angle the bullets passed through the body from end to end—this man was shot through lung and belly both.

The shrapnel was now only fired at long intervals and the road was open except for the sharp-shooters.

We sent a message to the Montenegrin doctors at Muričan for stretchers.

At ten Gospodin Michan came in by the road. The poor old man had journeyed up to find the Colonel and congratulate him on his victory.

I had just made a jugful of tea and called the others to it when I saw Mike in the yard, standing alone and exposed, prodding the ground with his stick. Cap was sitting on the bed, Lauder on the window-sill, nursing their cups, when he came up to us.

He stepped into the middle of the room and said "G'mornin' Cap, G'mornin' Lauder, G'mornin' Cary." Mike at Vilgar had been a handsome old man with firm lines in his cheek and jaw. Now his whole face was sagged, his eyes looked paler, his lip hung.

"Would you like to come see the Colonel's body?" he said, lifting his chin.

Cap went out with him.

Marcović came down shortly afterwards from the walls and Cap brought him in—to our loft.

We all drank tea together. Marcović's voice was gone altogether. He could only squeak, and as his French was bad at the best, it was hard to understand him.

He was untouched except for rips in his uniform made by the wire.

He told us that the redoubt and part of the trenches on each side of it were taken and held. The other parts of these trenches were empty and could be kept by either party. Since they were shallow, and built with a parapet on the down side, they afforded no protection except on that side. The Turks from the fort within the last circle of wire could shoot straight into them.

On the other hand the Montenegrins enfiladed them from the redoubt. It remained for the sappers to build walls on their upper sides before they could be occupied.

We heard that the Brigadier Gurnić was to be given the Colonel's command.

Gurnić we knew. He had been at Zogaj and arranged the gun positions and the camp there. We were glad that he was to take over the work at Tarabos, for we hoped to see the last fort taken.

Marcović was eager to do anything for us that he could. He sent a more urgent message to Muričan for stretchers, and promised that he would find men to carry them.

This relieved us of the worst of our anxieties.

The stable was piled with wounded and dead, and we had not known how to get them away even when the road should be safe enough. They had had no food now for more than twenty-four hours. It is true that each man was supposed to go into the fight with two days' rations, but few of them did. I made a couple of jugs of milk in the morning, about three gallons together, which we took round to all the worse off. Milk is best in such a case because it is compact to carry, and will do no harm to any sort of wound.

The fight continued all day in bursts of half an hour with a shell or two, and twenty minute pauses.

Few wounded came in, but there were always two of us at work, because many had to be redressed.

At four the first stretchers were sent away, and after that the road towards Muričan by way of the river-bed was safe enough for those that could walk. The firing decreased to no more than the usual sniping and an occasional thirty shot fusillade from the maxim—when a half battalion of reliefs filed in from Dramos, they found Crepaj very dull. It had the air of a room on the morning after a debauch, with spilt wine and empty bottles.

We left in the dark. There was a little column of us that marched out. Two or three stretchers led the way, each on the shoulders of four men, others beside them carrying the bearers' rifles.

Then came Cap, Lauder, and Borjo with a sack of dressings, I came last with a stick on my shoulder, and the lanterns tied to the end of it. Of course we shewed no light.

We marched fast to Dramos, then slower up and down the wide folds and dips of the hillsides.

Dramos was ablaze with camp fires below us as we went by. There was a high tower of yellow light in the middle and domes round it, like a flaming cathedral, with the vast dark landscape of the Bojana behind, and a strip of pale sea high up to the west. We marched between the mountains and this valley.

I fell several times, and my mind scarcely recorded the fact that I had been down and up again.

The column topped each next rise, one by one against the sky—first a bayonet or two, then the long cloaked soldiers, the stretchers, Cap quick and neat, still twirling his stick, Borjo very burly and rolling, Lauder with his head down, meditative—and disappeared. When I reached the top, and looked down into the hollow, there was nothing to be seen—I might have been alone, but for the rattle of Lauder's nailed boots on the stones.

Here and there we passed wounded men, resting in the dark—one or two smoking. Two or three who recognised us cried out, "Goodnight," as we went by. I do not think some of them got any further. We met also a woman or two waiting for their men.

Bobote was filling up when we came stumbling down the market place. There were reserves there and an ammunition party with their mules, as well as a crowd of wounded and many women. Women were always sent away from the front before a battle, but I think that some of them only went into hiding, and came out as soon as the fight started.

Grgić, a Montenegrin doctor, had been in charge of Bobote during the battle. He had already gone back to Muričan when we arrived, but the embers were warm on the hearth.

Cap and Lauder set to work to make themselves a rice pudding. I took off my puttees and lay down on my sack in the corner.

My last recollection was of the fire and the dixie, with Lauder and Cap gazing anxiously into it, while a maxim was rattling violently somewhere towards Tarabos.

Part Four

36

THE next morning I lit the fire, and drew the water and made the tea, and cut the bread for breakfast and cleaned the pan and waked Lauder. The serious part of war again involved us.

After breakfast the patients were seen, and after lunch we climbed over to Zogaj to make our report. There had been about seven hundred casualties. We had dressed rather more than five hundred wounded, and the dead were officially returned at one hundred and seventy.

Williams, Todd, and Starkie, veterans of the first battle, received us with invitations to bread and jam, the proper food of adventure. Doctor Goldsmith and Doctor Sherwin conferred meanwhile with Cap. We knew that Cap had long outstayed his leave in hopes of a fight, and were not surprised to hear that night on our return to Bobote that he was going back to India in three days. Dr. Sherwin was to command us.

We found out later the character that had been given to him of his lieutenant and orderly. He was told we were quarrelsome, especially Cookee—but could be made to quarrel with each other because we came from opposite ends of Ireland; that one of us had the notions of a Montenegrin who gets himself killed on purpose; the other was absent-minded enough to walk into the Turkish lines in a fit of philosophic speculation. This latter I think is meant for Lauder. He had a bad reputation, together with Todd and Williams, for straying about in the open, gained in the February battle.

Doc (on the analogy of Cap) said both applied to each of us, and refused to argue.

Cap left that week.

We all three climbed the ridge together towards Zogaj.

I shook hands there and came back, while they went on down.

I felt this break-up the more keenly that I spent the night alone and Bobote appeared to be twice over a miserable desert—no Cap and no

Lauder. Borjo supped and talked, but, for all that Borjo was a good fellow, his talk only reminded me of isolation—that my nearest comrade was divided from me by a point of view a thousand years apart, and a language at its closest in San Francisco.

But Lauder brought Dr. Sherwin over with him the next day and we set up house again.

Doc began by dispatching Lauder to Antivari to eat some good meals and get some sea air. My sack was put on Lauder's bed and I was ordered to get into it.

Doc meanwhile lit his own fires, cooked his own and my meals, saw all the sick, and went every day over to Zogaj for stores.

Doc is a middle-sized man with a short brown face and a short brown beard, short conversation, blue eyes, and a long endurance. When he was angry his beard stood up slightly with the contraction of his cheeks, beyond that there was nothing to tell by. He was as violent and tireless a marcher as Cap and rolled his puttees no less neatly, but lost more wind.

For three days he kept me in my sack lying a glorious invalid, smoking his own Pig's-face (or Negrohead), with my meals coming to me as easily as if I were a beast of the field, or a millionaire in an hotel. On the fourth I went back with relief to duty, and made a Bobote stew.

That night as we sat over the fire in grave meditation, the door was burst suddenly open and Lauder appeared. He carried a sack, which he spilled immediately upon the floor.

There was a tin of jam from Zogaj, six of squashed tomatoes from Virpazar, seven or eight potatoes, and a large round parcel for me.

"I found it at Antivari," said Lauder, looking at it on the floor. "I've had the devil of a time with it. It looks like shortbread."

He sat down and rolled a cigarette, Doc continued to smoke, both too polite to ask me to open the parcel.

When my own dottel was knocked out, Doc offered to lend me a knife, and since my own was on its lanyard and slung always about my neck, I took this for a hint.

The parcel held a large cake. It was burnt here and there, but that was a guarantee of home kneading and baking. We cut it in half and divided the half into three whacks of about eight ounces each—it had a fine tawny flesh, firm and just damp enough to keep the bites distinct,

while the currants and raisins were very evenly distributed at intervals of a centimetre, no desert places, no unfairly rich pockets to cause jealousy.

37

The news now from the trenches was that Gurnić meant to sap up to the third wire and the last fort, as Plomenatz had done in the case of the second, and the lower redoubt. The Turks' connecting trench could be used, but the parapet had to be shifted from one side to the other, several walls built on its flanks, and some deepening effected at the turns. It would take a fortnight. Meanwhile even the snipers were less enterprising after the fight, the gunners were saving ammunition for another assault, and there was no work for us.

Doc decided that we should go to the base for a day or two to eat some fresh meat and buy stores, while Lauder and Borjo, with Todd if he could be given leave from Zogaj, were left in charge.

We set out before breakfast—Lauder and the pup put their noses about three inches beyond the blankets to wish us good-bye—and climbed the mountain in the cool of early morning.

At Zogaj we ate, and went from that to Skla to catch the steamer down the lake.

The mosque at Zogaj stands at the water's edge, so that stores could be brought right to its steps in the Albanian galleys, while even a steamer came up once in February to take away the wounded. But the steamer was shelled and never dared beyond Skla again. The wounded were carried from Zogaj to Skla in galleys and left on Skla beach if the steamer had not come. We could have waited to hail a boat, but we chose to march.

Skla is a little harbour among the hills, with three or four cottages, and some terraced farms.

There was a store-house there to which rice, beans and bread, bacon-fat, and ammunition were brought from the base, to be sent on to all the battalions south of the lake.

It was just opposite Reoli, on the north shore, which supplied Vukotić's army. The steamers made generally a round of Rjeka, Virpazar, Reoli, Skla, Plavnitza, Virpazar again, and Rjeka. Skla beach was always in a bustle.

The mosque at Zogaj stands at the water's edge ... (opposite page)

There were soldiers come for their company-rations, flag-men supervising, and artillery officers looking after their ammunition, Albanian boatmen waiting to unload (there was no pier at Skla), peddlers, women going home each with a pack on her back and an umbrella, and the wounded and sick.

Doc and I sat down on a stone, pared off a fill of Pig's-face and lit our pipes.

After an hour the steamer was sighted; by another half-hour she was in harbour. She brought a barge with her, which was pulled close enough to the beach for direct unlading.

The soldiers and Albanians splashed to and fro in the shallows with boxes, sacks, and shells. The shells were dispatched at once to the guns, the three inch carried by one man, the six inch shared between two. Bread was piled into boats and rowed away toward Zogaj, while other loaves were divided into heaps on the stones of the beach.

Doc and I settled ourselves upon the upper deck skylight where the funnel would warm us in the evening. We had the ordinary outlook upon fantastic mountains and islands during the journey, mountains growing colder and seeming to retreat further and further into an austere privacy of their own as the evening advanced; islands standing one head above water and in the stars, the other below in those same stars reflected.

I was left in Virpazar, and slept at the old mother's; Doc polished his buttons and went on to Cettinje.

This was Thursday and the next day was the market-day of Virpazar. The old mother came in with the jug at seven to wash me, and my coffee-milk was then already made. I went out to watch the country people coming over the water—their boats could be seen a mile away on the smooth sea, then to come winding through the tops of the willow trees. The rowers were all women; the men were at the front. They greeted each other at a hundred yards distance, vigorously pushing at their oars with cries of "Good morning, madam." "This is a fine day." "Good day, madam, how are you?" "Well, madam, this is a fine morning. What are you bringing to market?"

The boats were tied up beside the meat-shop. I breakfasted at the station café, where there is an Austrian woman who speaks French and makes omelettes.

She had a tablecloth too; little carafons of wine with the glasses inverted on their mouths like tooth-water glasses; two or three knives and forks to each place; napkins; a glass affair in the middle of the table—I sat on a chair and Madame came round to my left side in order to offer me the omelette. No more could be done at the Ritz.

After breakfast I went to market; found a Turk and the Mexican rebel (who had got leave by some old soldier's ruse) to carry sacks, and bought the stores—tea, matches, a lamp chimney for Zogaj, five hundred ready-made cigarettes, tinned tomatoes, onions, potatoes, five strings of figs, sixty loaves of white bread, pepper and salt, two pots of mustard and seven oranges—all there were. Lastly I bargained for a lamb in the meat-shop, closed for eleven crowns, and had it slung above the stairs in the old mother's against the departure of the boat.

This boat was to have come at five on Saturday.

I rose at half past four. The old mother, who always herself got up at four, saw to it that I was turned out. When I tried to sleep she began to wash me in the bed with cold water. From ten minutes to five till seven I sat on an old gun at the quay.

At seven, omelette.

Seven to nine, sun and meditation.

At nine, omelette and conference with Governor. (No boat to-day, by Jesus).

Nine to half past eleven, visit to the citadel, where the guard turned out and gave me a drink of wine, shocking sour wine drunk from a very dirty-mouthed bottle, but they were old friends of Starkie's and mine in our Virpazar days and liked to do me honour.

I said it was magnificent wine and asked if it was the Colonel's. (From Colonel Plomenatz' vineyard—the best wine). They did not know where it came from but were flattered by my compliment, and one old man offered to bring out another bottle. He was nudged so violently by the others, however, that it was plain they had no more, and my polite refusal, which under ordinary circumstances would have been badly received, was now held very considerate.

At this moment I looked over the battlements and saw a steamer coming down the gulf.

"That steamer is for Reoli?" I asked.

"Otch-Otch, Reoli i Skla, gospodin." Yes, Reoli and Skla, sir.

I threw myself down the mountain-side, charged along the road, and arrived on the quay as the steamer was warped in.

"Where are you going to?" I shouted to the captain.

"Nowhere," he answered, "we stay."

12. Lunch, soup, meat, fried potatoes, macaroni and fried meat, coffee.

1. More coffee with the Governor.

1.15. Inspection of lamb to see how it is keeping.

1.20 to 7. Furious marching and counter-marching all over all the mountains, rocks, canyons, cliffs of the known world, hands in pockets, hands swinging, hands climbing, hands clasped behind, hands waggling from thumbs stuck into braces—with meditations, contemplations, reflections, compositions, songs, speeches, whistling, duologues, in which the other parts were severally taken up by Gregor, Panurge, Heneage, Doctor Pangloss, Mr Micawber, Brierly, Lauder, Pope Pius, Mord Emly, the Nigger of the Narcissus, Harry Richmond, Epistemon, The Knight of the Burning Pestle and the Nuremberg Man.

7.0. Dinner at a friend of the old mother's—smashed chickens.

8.0. A coffee with the Mexican at the Blue house by the bridge.

9.0. Bed, and at

10.0. The steamer went out; the old mother came to tell me of it; no one seemed to know where she was bound for.

On Sunday I sat again upon the gun from nine to twelve and smoked the top off my tongue, sinking at last into a sort of Buddhist condition of mind which is either the cellar or garret of existence, no one can tell which.

At one I heard definitely by message from the Governor that there was to be no boat.

A launch came in at 1.15 with Doc, but I was told it was to go back immediately to Rjeka.

Doc had found his sister in Cettinje and was bound for Antivari with her by the train. I went to see them off and was negligently leaning out of the carriage window, watching the energetic arguments of an Albanian Mallissori family, when the Town Marshal suddenly came to attention before me and declared, "Boat for Skla in seven minutes."

I ran furiously through the crowd, over the bridge, and up the market-place, roaring Turski at short intervals. There were four of them at my heels by the time I reached the old mother's, broad, lumbering, grave Redifs, heavy of body and spindly of leg.

They made very light work of the sacks, and trotted them all to the boat in less than six minutes. I carried the lamb under my arm.

When those sacks were piled, the Turks paid off and I myself perched solidly on the heap, I looked to see the hawsers cast off within the half minute. I sat there for half an hour before the engine-man had even finished his hoosh-koosh and then he was kept for another ten minutes by an affray with three stevedores on the quay.

We came to Skla in the dusk, creeping close up past the islands and sliding secretively into the harbour.

From Skla to Zogaj was the hardest stretch for a transport-master.

The last man that brought stores before me (an Irishman, it was not Lauder) left Virpazar even richer laden than I, and arrived at Zogaj with nothing but a haversack full of roast chestnuts. He had been marooned and God knows what happened to his sacks.

I stood by my heap therefore, and looked out.

Two galleys began the unlading. The engine-man suggested that they had room for me, but I knew that private stores landed at Skla in the dark were lost stores, and I refused the engine-man.

It looked at last as if I should be left on board and carried to Reoli, when a small boat suddenly came round the point with a wounded man.

As he was put on board I hailed them in Serb. "Are you from Zogaj?"

"Yes, *sir*," said one in Yankee.

"And going back?"

"Shure."

"I have four sacks here for the English doctors."

"We take them, shure."

The sacks were pitched in, and I put myself on the broad overhang of the bow. One of the men rolled up his cloak for me to sit on.

We rowed three oars, one steering, one pulling, one pushing. The men sang, chaffed, gossiped always in English out of politeness to myself, unless the words failed. It was decided that "Son-of-a-bitch Owstria worse than the Dagos." "Wine too much watered at Fishing-House" and after enquiry from me about prices at Bobote, "Too damn dear to charge double price for mountain" (for taking over the mountain). "The Colonel was fine man, good man. What for did they let him get killed?" "Turski good fighting men—son-of-bitches."

When conversation flagged for the first time I was asked:

"How you like dis country? Pretty pore, I guess."

"It's a fine country."

"How long you bin dis country?"

"Five months."

"Yes, sir? You talk Montenegrin."

"Otch-otch male, bogami." (Yes a little, by God).

At this they all repeated "Bo-gami dobra" and laughed.

"You from Zogaj?"

"From Bobote."

"You was at Crepaj, shure. You see my brudder. He was wounded in head by mitrailleuse (maxim) second day in the morning." And they broke into discussion of the battle that lasted out the journey.

The mosque was lighted up as we came by the rocks.

They stopped rowing and I hailed.

The shouts echoed over the desolation of ruined cottages, and broken hill-side, but no one came.

We ran the boat in and landed the stores ourselves. These soldiers scrambled about in the water and stumbled over the rocks with my sacks, all for kindness. I mentioned the word drinks to them as they embarked to see if they could be paid. I received instead an invitation to the Fishing-House for nine o'clock to coffee and wine. I was obliged to refuse on the score that I might have to climb the mountain for Bobote that night.

They rowed off towards the camp and I went up to the house to find Doctor Goldsmith.

"Where's the bread?" asked Doctor Goldsmith with anxiety.

"At the mosque, sir."

"Go to the Sergeant-Major and ask for your supper."

The Zogaj kitchen was a gay place compared to the dreary magnificence of the station café of Virpazar (there is a looking-glass and an overmantle in that café). I sat down between Williams and Ford at the table and ate macaroni pudding and was waited upon by Malé (daughter of the Zogaj washerwoman) with all the conscious worthiness of a man that has brought white bread.

I lay on the floor at the mosque and watched their scoundrelly interpreter, Elia, come in drunk from the Fishing-House, yet sensible enough to spread a newspaper by his bed for ease of spitting during the night, and went to sleep by the noise of the ripple on the stones.

38

Todd had been three days in Bobote to keep Lauder company. Todd of course was himself a Bobote by descent, right, and invitation. He was the Minister Plenipotentiary of the Bobotes at Zogaj to watch over · the rightful sharing of onions and potatoes, enduring luxury that we might escape starvation. He might be expected about ten o'clock any morning with a sack (wheedled from the Sergeant-Major) full of milk and meat (probably stolen). He would look into the dixie to see what was for lunch, seat himself with the careful slowness which all big men use towards furniture, light a cigarette, tip his cap over his forehead, screw up his eyes and elevate his beard to watch the smoke of the fire, and remain fixed in meditation. After ten minutes, as if struck by a new thought, he would twist himself about to look at the soles of his boots to find out what further splits, hones and flaps had been cut by the morning's mountain, and remark in a blood-to-the-head tone, "I suppose there's enough stew to go round, Cookee?"

Sometimes in a conversational mood he might remind me, "You remember that journey with the pony and Vuko from Vilgar?"

To which I always answered "My God!" and we both gazed solemnly at the hearth for a moment.

In the same way, if any of Leake's first party (Lauder, Todd, or Williams) should say, "D'you remember that smell at Pentari?" the others would answer, "Good Lord!" or "Good God!" and fall into contemplative attitudes.

I, who had not been at Pentari at the time of the smell, would be made impatient by this sort of reminiscence, as we were all likely to be impatient with Lauder when he would begin—"I remember how in Tripoli, when one of those Dago airships"—or, "You should have seen the pup I had out in Tripoli; cleverest little beast you could imagine. I remember," etc., etc. Part of Lauder in fact, the Tripoli part, was in exile among us.

What is an exile—he is a man to whom no tree or hedge or face or hill or room or river ever can say "D'you remember?" and cause his heart to reply "Good God!" He is a sad fellow. At least let any man driven far abroad take a list of place names with him—say Peggy Elkins, Saltpans, Porta Doris, Fisherman's leap, the Tuns, Magilligan point, the Metal Man, Dumbie's Harbour, or such like—to sit round the fire (or where there are no fires, opposite the cigars) with him at night and make him feel that he is own brother or, at furthest, cousin to reality and not merely the burst bladder of an unmoored balloon.

So one-tree-pass, Zogaj, Vilgar, Muričan, the mulberry tree, tie me and tied all of us by added ropes to the delightful world—and Bobote too; so I return to Bobote.

But when I came in that morning, the room might have suffered a bombardment or a siege—an inch of dirt, empty tins, charred twigs, splinters, ash, and cigarette ends on the floor, the plates and cups in all sorts of nonchalant attitudes, and the dixies both burnt black. The pup was sucking the lid of a bully can; Borjo was frying bread; Lauder was squatting next him with a cigarette, one puttee on, one still in his hand; Todd was sounding the ribs of a battered flag-man in the background.

I was saluted by a sleepy smile from Lauder and a muffled shout of "Hullo Cook—ee!" from somewhere behind the flag-man's sheepskins.

While we cleaned house, sweeping, plate-washing, scouring, a leg of the lamb was roasted.

Recipe—Take the worst of your dixies. Melt an inch of bacon-fat in it. Baste the lamb with fat also and put it into the dixie with some sliced onion, over a clear small fire. As soon as the fat begins to fry throw in a cupful of water. After an hour or so turn the leg over and put in another cupful of water, if necessary.

We made a good lunch and went down the hill to talk politics and scandal and watch the shells burst at intervals on Tarabos (waiting each time for a reply, and if none came, deciding for the hundredth time that the Turk's ammunition was running out) while the sun shone, the stream ran, the flies buzzed, and the pup looked for snakes in the bushes.

It was this day on our return for supper the sentry gave me a note,

Gentlemen of the Red Cross Boboty a letter at the Murichan Post Office awaiting Mr. J. [undecipherable] Kary or Cary.
Yours Very Truly
S. N. Mitrovitch
of Zoganje.
On route to Murichan will stop here on my way back to-morrow—

from in fact the old San Franciscan interpreter (great foe of Borjo's) called "the Professor" in Zogaj.

He brought me the letter next day and I read it as I stirred the stew—the potstick in my right hand, pipe in mouth, a regiment of lice wriggling on every rib—it dealt mainly with the Insurance Act, and how it might affect the Bye-Elections.

39

The blockade of Antivari always continued. We could see the ships from Bobote, and it amused the old men sitting on the gallery to point at them when we passed and cry out, "English ships." We had to explain many times, with grave earnestness, that we did not countenance the action of our Government.

At this time, after the Crepaj battle, we were always expecting the Austrians. Every day there was a rumour that they were on the march. We knew that they were concentrated on the frontiers, and that Italy had also thirty thousand men mobilized. It was held in Bobote market-place that if the Italians came it would be only a check to Austria.

The incident of Lovchen was not forgotten.

Lovchen is the Montenegrin mountain which dominates Cattaro. Cattaro is an Austrian port, and would be one of the best naval ports of the Adriatic—with a natural channel deep enough for any Dreadnought, an inner harbour with anchorage for half a dozen capital ships, and impregnable defences, if it were not for Lovchen. From Cattaro streets one can see the Montenegrin forts six hundred feet above, and there is only one possible road to the summit. When in the middle of the war Russia refused to send any more corn or guns to Nicholas, and Italy also threatened to be hostile, Nicholas made overtures to Austria with Lovchen as a consideration for their help. It was unlikely that he was serious, but Russia and Italy at once came to heel. Italy could not allow Austria to have Lovchen and a naval port so far down the Adriatic as Cattaro; Russia does not wish to see Austria more powerful at the expense of a Balkan State, one of those States that it is hoped will obey Russia.

More guns, corn, and ammunition arrived; the Italian plenipotentiary became polite.

So that it was supposed very fairly that the Italian troops were mobilized more for a check than a help. But we looked for the blue coats and grey stockings of Austria every morning, and wondered how they would fare in the swamps of Pentari and the mountains of Shiroska.

40

Doc came back in three days bringing jam and cigarette papers, and put us in a whirl of energy at once. We did not go to our nest in the gully any more—one day to the batteries on the mountain, the next to Oblique, the third to Muričan. None of these journeys taught us very much. At Oblique we found new guns, twelve to fifteen centimetre howitzers from Russia, in new positions by the Bojana river, from which they flanked Brditza to a certain extent. At Muričan we saw the General, and asked to be allowed to go with two battalions we had seen that day on the march—they were to take the Servians' places before Brditza—but were told to stay where we were and be ready for another assault. In fact there was promise of another battle but nothing to be done for the present.

The pup lost herself on the Muričan journey, and caused Lauder some uneasiness. He waited two days, and then marched back alone to find her.

She was with a lover. Lauder did not at all approve of the match, describing the bridegroom as a black mongrel, lame in the hind leg, with a broken tail, and forbade the banns. The pup nevertheless grieved for a few hours, and then worked off her trouble in prolonged efforts to get a four inch skull into a three inch meat-tin.

Lauder watched her from his box by the hearth (we were already in our sacks—smoking last pipes in the grave presence of our own marvellous giant shadows, which imitated our movements on the walls, as if only to teach us how with the same muscles and features we could be ten times as grave and dignified) and obviously forgave her all his anxieties and rough miles of counter-marching.

We were all in forgiving mood at those nights of Bobote. During the day we were apt to be very outspoken, grousing and growling at each other, or inventing chaff with a sting to it, bent on our own business and scornful of other people's. But after dinner, Lauder often wiped the plates, Cap patted the puppy, or I was polite to Borjo, and we sat by the fire and went to bed full of moderately kind thoughts for each other.

Doc is out of this argument because I don't think he ever had any but kind thoughts of the whole created world, which would make many men's lives very dull, but did not seem to depress Doc.

This air of live-and-let-live was due partly to our being tired, and fed, and ready to sleep, partly to the sacred influence of home.

It is hard to describe the full delight of one's own fireside and one's own house to people that have never had a fireside or a house of their own.

We had not a house of our own in the strict sense, because we found it ready built. We could not enjoy our house so much as the soldiers who lived in the straw huts next door, and had contrived them for themselves, did theirs. But the fire was our own, every stick, and the furniture was our own to the last sugar-box. I made two hanging cupboards for the drugs, out of packing-cases, that gave me more pleasure to look at than Sheraton or Chippendale.

This is not meant for a paradox. You who sit in an armchair, made by a man you don't know the name of, and bought in a shop, before a fire of coals dug out by total strangers in a country as far off, for all you care, as Kamtchatka, delivered at your door by a heaver at best merely an acquaintance, arranged and lit by a servant who probably does not greatly like you, do not know what the pleasure of the fireside means. Again, though I had not made my sleeping-sack (the better if I had) I had watched over it, guarded it, trundled it about, shouldered it over the hills, until it had at least the status of a comrade, if not altogether a child of my own fashioning.

Lauder's bed was the white elephant of camp after camp; it was crooked, ramshackle, creaking, bagged in the middle, unsafe, but he would sooner have deserted his pup than it; indeed long after the pup was lost and Bobote deserted, I was specially commissioned to find it for him, pack it over the mountains on mule-pack, convey it to Scutari by galley, and tranship it to Virpazar, Cettinje, Cattaro, Trieste, Milan, Paris, London, Holyhead, to the county Cork, where now it probably lies in a lumber-room; and this bed was only a friend. If we could have conveyed our fire and furniture to Ireland, sugar-boxes, hearth-stone, faggots, the pseudo-Chippendale cabinets, the bayonet-candlestick, and set up house with them there, we should live more at home now than anyone since Diogenes, and I doubt if he coopered his own keg, or

Tolstoy, and I know most of his primitive furniture had to be made in Paris in order to be of correct early pattern. The birds are nearly the last householders left.

41

We went again to Oblique after this parley with the General, to find out how the new guns were doing (a bombardment had been going on for several days—echoed distantly in Bobote) and to guess how they would affect the plans of another assault.

We marched by the Dramos road, scuttled over the Tom Tiddler's land of Crepaj into the river-bed, and came to Oblique for lunch with Mam'selle and M'sieu, who were as quarrelsome with each other as ever and polite in an equal proportion to everyone else. The fiercer the altercation, by that the more hospitable to their guests.

We went from them to the Chief Officer of Artillery and found him out, but we met the Count Catapani.

This Count is an adventurous journalist who had by some means got himself promoted to a kind of honorary A.D.C.-ship to one of the Brigadiers.

He is married to an American and speaks English. Lauder knew him from old days. There was a famous row at Medua with him which no one ever forgot and General Martinović liked especially to remember.

I was not there. The parties were Cap, Todd, Lauder, Warden, and Williams on the one hand, then starting upon their long journey up to Bojana which brought them to Vilgar, and Catapani with his Boy Scouts on the other.

The Boy Scouts were supposed to be a Red Cross unit, but they were of very tender years besides being armed to the teeth. They were sent home after three weeks' glorious career which ended in the repulse of an imaginary night-attack (said to be a goat by some, a mule by others) with so much random rifle-and-revolver fire that the General thought them too dangerously brave for their responsible position.

There was at Medua only one room fit for a field hospital, which the British immediately seized. Catapani claimed this room by every title; he had reached Medua first; he had a larger contingent; the Commandant of Medua had given it him; but he failed by any means to dislodge the brigands in possession.

After a last stormy tirade he walked fiercely out, and had already passed the door, when he remembered the repartee he was looking for. He shot his head round the jamb, fixed the party with his glittering spectacles and roared, "Damn London!"

We found him in a lieutenant's uniform, very new, and a pair of tortoiseshell glasses, his moustache brushed upwards, and his cap over the left eye. He was an important man, even it is said a political agent.

He talked excellent three-decker English of the Johnsonian sort, in a high sing-song voice—like the famous comedian who danced a horn-pipe in fetters. His news covered all the scandals, bankruptcies, divorce cases, abductions, Tammany briberies, English perfidies, Italian military greatnesses of several years, with digressions into literature, art, and music. It would be hard to find a man who was so violently determined to impress—and gave himself to such strange methods of finger-snapping, prancing, moustache-twirling, strutting, now looking down his nose from the full height of five feet six, now brushing an imaginary fly off his shoulder strap, again cocking out his leg, supporting his left elbow on his right hand and patting his cheek with his left, while the polysyllables (accents shaky) flew out of him like ballet dancers with rheumatics.

But in the end we came to the important fact he was keeping for a plum, that the Brditza bridge was broken, smashed at four thousand yards range by a shell from the fifteen centimetre, and the Turks cut in half. Brditza you can see on my map [p. 107]. It was a very strong position. The Servians made no impression on it at all. It was steep and splendidly entrenched, while the approaches were all bogs and swamps. There was water round two sides of it. It was cut off by the Bojana from Tarabos and by the Drinassa from Scutari; there were two bridges, one between Scutari and Tarabos, another between Scutari and Brditza. It was the latter, a structure mostly of wood, that was now knocked down.

We parted from the Count with hand-shakes of the usual Continental earnestness, a firm grip, a bend forward from the hips, a dropping of the voice, a turning up of the eyes.

Borjo also had news for us. He came in after supper to tell us that an envoy had gone in to Scutari that day by boat and several Turkish officers came out, and that they had held a parley with Martinović and Vukotić at Skla.

We were waked next morning by the ammunition mules. The stable beneath our room, I had forgot to say, was a magazine, where rifles, bombs, and ammunition were kept. It was amusing to watch the drivers raking their grenades out of our piles of empty bully cans and milk tins. Ten mule loads of cartridges were taken that morning and sent forward to Tarabos.

The rumour was of a failure in negotiation and another general assault. We began to look over our stores. Two wounded men (one shot in the belly, but mending) who had been lying in the other room on improvised beds of pack-saddles and sheepskins, were sent on stretchers to Zogaj.

I counted loaves, milk, and meat. Lauder went over his drugs and bandages, while Doc saw the morning's patients. Borjo was sent to Zogaj with two orderlies and a note for dressings and rations.

42

Borjo waked us at half past six to say that the battalions were already on the march.

We had a perambulating breakfast, carrying fried bread in one hand, packing with the other, seized our wood-and-water orderly, a taciturn ragamuffin already dozing on the wood pile with his rifle between his knees, gave him a sack of dressings, and started him away. Ourselves followed in ten minutes, at a little before seven o'clock, with the last of the emergency rations in our haversacks and water-bottles full of cold tea.

We took the way of the goat-track for short cut and caught our orderly with no more than a few bruises; but the battalion had a long start. Lauder carried the pup after the first half mile.

We toiled up the rise for Dramos about eight, Doc, Lauder, Borjo, Vuko (orderly), and I, and one by one we stopped at the top, till we made a group—Doc a little in front. Before us stood the whole Cettinski Battalion drawn up in two lines, twenty yards apart, facing in. At the far end stood Captain Martinović, their Commandant, the General's brother—a man of six feet two, with the scarlet and white standard and the flag-man beside him. The company flags were also in their places.

We had watched for a moment or so, when there was a noise of horses and the General rode up with his staff.

Our small group saluted, and Martinović waved his hand to us.

He rode then between the lines to his brother at the far end, who stood gravely at attention.

Martinović shook hands with him, then turned and shouted for a cheer for the king. The Battalion roared. Immediately they were closed up and began the advance by companies. We followed the Battalion flag-man.

The Komerskozagaratchski had been waiting at Crepaj and joined us on the hillside.

We passed the broken wire of the February battle, many small graves, many little shelters full of spent cases. There was a sweet sickly smell of dead unburied bodies. When we reached the forward walls of the old outpost we were made take cover. As the order was passed back from flag-man to flag-man, the companies sank down in succession, the padding and rustling of hundreds of moccasins ceased, and there was a sudden dead silence.

The flags, each a burning patch of scarlet against brown cloaks and grey rocks, moved a little in the light wind, but the soldiers sat motionless, their bayonets standing up in a stiff bristle, their faces turned, row behind row, towards the summit.

For three or four minutes this continued. Suddenly a small figure stepped out against the sky on the parapet of the Turkish fort, and stood. No one yet moved or made any noise; we all stared at that small dark silhouette on the crown of the hill for thirty seconds in a kind of catalepsy. Martinović walked out with two officers and climbed. The staff, the ensign of the Cettinski, and ourselves followed—behind, the whole hillside was in movement with the battalions, their bayonets and their flags.

The Turkish officer was a neat little man in green and gold. He wore a dark green mourning turban in place of a kalpak. His guard of six Nizami in full marching kit stood behind. Martinović shook hands with him and they turned down towards the first gun. I found myself one of a group of Turkish soldiers stumbling over the stones and broken pieces of shell after the long stride of the Montenegrin and the lively step of the little Turk.

It was a term of the surrender that all the siege guns should be handed over in fighting condition.

The Nizami re-formed behind the gun, then their corporal pulled the cover off its breech block. A Montenegrin gunner stooped, glanced at the screws, opened and shut the block, stepped back and saluted.

The Turkish officer was crying. He bent down and kissed the gun, and each of his soldiers followed him in turn.

It is noteworthy that when the gun was handed over, some of the companies coming up the hill began to cheer, and immediately half a dozen men near me turned round to hush them. There was no cheering. The flags were all the show of triumph.

We went on from gun to gun. At each there was a small guard who, as soon as the gun was formally delivered up, turned down the flanks of the hill and made for the Scutari bridge. Martinović and the Turk were always in front, the General talking and striding, the Turk gesticulating and skipping over the stones.

We climbed Little Tarabos at half past one—by two o'clock the last trench was seen and the Turkish officer hurried off towards the town with his six men. Probably they were picked men, but for all their wasted looks they were good-looking soldiers.

The Battalions all sat down on the round top of Little Tarabos and ate their rations.

From Little Tarabos both the Scutaris can be seen, the old and the new. The old is the native bazaar. It stands on the water's edge and is joined to Tarabos by a long iron bridge over the Bojana. The new town is about a mile and a half away. It covers a great deal of space, because every house, except the shops in the main street, is surrounded by its garden.

Between the old town and the new there are commons and a good road.

As we sat on Tarabos we watched the Turkish regiments marching slowly down the road, disappearing into the bazaar and appearing again in a great crowd at the side of the broken bridge to Brditza. From this they were ferried over in small boats, and could be seen straggling down the road past Brditza and Barbalucki towards Medua and the sea.

Two-thirds of their regulars died in this siege, and three-quarters of the officers. Where the great part of an army consists of irregular troops, casualties among the regular regiments and the officers will always be proportionately large. The officers must expose themselves more, both because they have more to do and because they must be more often seen by their men, while the regular troops will have to take the hardest share of fighting.

We were in the middle of bully and biscuits when the General came over to us with his staff. We thrust the bully into our pockets and stood up, expecting an order of some sort. But Martinović made us a little complimentary speech, speaking in Serb instead of French, so that the soldiers might understand. Borjo extracted the gist of it for us, but it had an Eastern touch about it, even in the compressed form, that would not look well in cold print. We assured him that we had enjoyed the war very much, congratulated him on the fall of the town, and there was general hand-shaking—he went off towards Shiroska village below, and we sat down and disentangled our meat from the various other odds and ends in our pockets.

We decided to make a private attempt on Scutari as soon as we could get away. The enthusiasm of this resolve, which was blown up to a great height by the enthusiasm of the day itself and the contagious happiness of the army, was damped for a moment by the loss of the pup. Lauder whistled and shouted to no purpose. We held an informal inquiry—she had been seen with the lid of the bully can, always her favourite dish, just before the General came up. Lauder believed she had been kidnapped but we were sceptical. It was not credible that any-one in his senses would have stolen the puppy. We thought she had been frightened by the sudden standing up of the soldiers, and bolted, or fallen off the cliff in pursuit of a fly, or returned to her friend at Murican—or discovered an edible Turk. But we knew that we could probably get past the watch, in the broken ground, and hoped then to be able to send a message to the English doctors of the Red Crescent in the town, Russell, Hattersly, and Stathers.

We went down a goat track to the river-side, dodging the pickets, and worked along unchallenged to the bridge-head.

There was no one in sight, and we were already at the bridge next the guard-house, when a Turkish officer suddenly started out of it and accosted us, while a couple of Redifs followed him and stood to attention. He spoke to us in French and asked what we were doing. Doc and I explained and asked if he had an orderly who could take a message to the doctors. We pretended an anxiety about them which left the little captain quite unmoved. He told us politely that no one was to pass the bridge till three the next day, and no messages could go in.

We marched off discomforted and set out along the shore for Zogaj.

We were all worn out with the walking of the day, and the shore path through the villages on the South side of Scutari lake is nothing but a rough track of stones. My boots had been smashed to pieces long ago and I had to lift my right foot six inches high at every step and give a kick, in order to straighten the sole underneath it.

Lauder and Doc stayed at Shiroska village and I did not wait to see what they were doing. I came past the lower guns into Zogaj about seven, past the camp and the little bay with its longships drawn up on the shingle, through the turbaned stones of the graveyard, to the house at last.

Doctor Goldsmith met me on the steps and sent me at once to the Sergeant-Major for a meal.

Doc and Lauder came in half an hour later, and Lauder catching me on the balcony told me in a whisper that Doc had called a council in the graveyard for after supper.

I went down after supper towards the mosque and chose a big head-stone for a seat. A gentle hail of "Cookee" in ten minutes or so warned me of the others coming.

I heard that at Shiroska they had stopped to call on the General, who promised to take us into the town if we were in time to catch his launch in the morning. The launch was to leave Shiroska at seven. Doc had arranged with Medoona, one of the old ladies who kept the mosque clean, for boiled eggs and coffee at a little past six.

After that I went to dress my foot and to bed. Lauder and Doc disappeared towards the Fishing-House for a bottle of wine.

43

When next day not only had I dressed in silence, but kicked up Lauder without waking the Zogaj sentinels that slept round us, and was already cautiously descending the ladder, Williams waked with customary suddenness, began to laugh, and then stopped as quickly when he saw me.

"Hullo! young Cary," he said.

"Hullo! Williams."

"Where are you going to?"

My chin was now at the level of the floor. I looked solemnly at Williams' disturbed face for a moment and then answered:

"Just going along." If Williams had asked, "Where to, young Cary?"

that would have started another conversation, but while he was still considering my answer from every side, I went away to get hot water for a new sore foot of Lauder's and my own old one.

Doc meanwhile fretted among the tombstones at the delay of Medoona.

It was a fine morning. The lake was covered with small running waves very eager to reach the shore, and there collapsing in most feeble tumbles. When Lauder and I had tied each other up, and Medoona had at last appeared, her face wrinkled like a beach at low tide, her mouth puckered in the effort of holding a very papery cigarette, and laid our breakfast on a flat tomb, we were tempted to linger over it much too long.

Williams and Ford indeed came down in time to catch us, but since we were then ready to go we did not hesitate to tell them we were bound for Scutari, as we slung our haversacks over our shoulders, waved Medoona farewell, and marched off.

The General's launch had left when we reached Shiroska; we were a quarter of an hour late for it, but a five miles forced march over the rocks with sore feet had already sobered our hopes, and when we found a table on the shore with wine, tea, and coffee selling, we sat down to rest and drink.

The three women who sold the coffee had rowed twenty miles from Virpazar that morning, in a little unhandy boat, bringing a table, three stools, and their own bedding and provisions. They looked perfectly neat, fresh, and cheerful as they sat knitting by their stall.

Other boats arrived while we were there, with similar parties. The first demand of all was for news of the surrender, and then of their own brothers and husbands.

We stayed an hour lounging and then went on to look for our battalion. We found the Cettinski flag-man halted half a mile this side of the bridge and made ourselves a nest in the neighbouring brake for lunch.

Here Borjo joined us, and Vuko, the orderly, the taciturn, who was now carrying his sack of dressing for the second day with grave fidelity, whereas when he had come on duty he had supposed himself a wood-and-water orderly with no work but to steal a few faggots from the other piles in the village, fetch a bucket or two from the well, and sit dozing all day by our door with his rifle across his knees. He had slept under a rock near by, and had been watching for us since dawn.

The flag went on at two and we followed with the battalion to the bridge-head. Here were the staff and a crowd of other notabilities.

We sat down again on the bridge wall to wait. A few gypsy children were wandering about among the soldiers, who fed them. They were wasted to the bone these children, like all the poorer children of Scutari.

At half past two the military police were sent in—not more than a hundred and fifty all told—to keep order in the bazaar.

We were expecting the staff to follow and the Cettinski flag-man, when an A.D.C. from Martinović asked if we would like to go in at once, watch the entry, and pick up our flag when it came over.

We jumped off our wall and marched off; Doc, Lauder, and myself in line, Borjo and Vuko behind, with their bayonets fixed.

There was a great crowd at the far end, with an open lane through it. Three Turks in civil dress, frock coats, and red fezzes, stood alone in the middle to receive us.

The band struck up. The gravest of the Turks stood out with a tray on which were a jug of wine and a cup. We exchanged salutes and drank each a cup of wine, saluted again, and passed down the lane between the band and the mob.

There was a house at the first corner which overlooked the whole bridge.

We tried the door. The Albanians near bolted right and left as if we were going for murder. Essad Pasha had told them that they would all be murdered when the Montenegrin army entered the town.

The door was opened by an old fellow in the last stage of panic. The place was a sort of store-house, of course empty at the moment. We went up a ladder to the second storey and found a window that gave on the bridge. The staff came riding over with their band and the big standard.

Martinović and Vukotić are both of a height, more than six feet three, and were mounted on very tall horses. They rode side by side; the staff followed and the long columns behind. Their march was reflected in the lake beneath to the very swords of the lieutenants.

The generals stopped at the bridge-head for their wine (the chief Turk most violently creased his frock-coat in the effort of lifting the tray high enough) and then rode on.

We ran down and fell in by the standard. At first the course lay through the bazaar, from one small alley to another, covered by the eaves of the houses, which shut out the sky all but a strip of a foot wide. The crowds peered in silence from the dark caverns of the open stalls. Every man and woman of them expected massacre that nightfall, but their attitudes and looks expressed for the most part nothing but indifference made easy by famine.

We found the sun again when we marched out on the road across the common. Those women who feared to be killed in the dark holes of the bazaar were sitting here in groups, their faces turned inwards, dressed all in their brightest colours, just as after the Antivari explosion.

But there was a great band of the foreign children drawn up by the road, with an enormous dragoman standing before them, wearing an Arab fez with the blue tassel and holding up the tricolor.

The children piped out their cheers and threw flowers over us. They stood on tiptoe in the effort of throwing their flowers over the tall ragged soldiers who brushed past. I was five yards to the right of the column and got my legs mixed up with some of the most excited of them.

We halted in the big barrack square of the new town. Martinović made a short speech, telling the men they were on honour to behave themselves, and the entry was over.

44

There was a beer-booth in a garden near the barrack-square, where we found plenty of Nikšić lager.

While we were at a second glass, Starkie and Todd walked in, and we drank together. The matter already to be debated was—when would the Austrians march; so that the fall of the town did not altogether bring us to humdrum level. It was not much doubted then by the troops that the Austrians would march. It was scarcely conceivable to a Montenegrin soldier that any nation should talk so much, parade so many troops, and make so many threats, without fighting at least a little in the end.

We had none of us more news than any other and went out, when the march was washed from our tongues, to look for quarters.

We met Hattersly, of the Red Crescent, at the first turn.

The three doctors of the Red Crescent had been living in the English

House, the Engleska Kuća, lent them by Captain Paget. We agreed to take a reversion of it the next morning. Captain Paget was not a party to the transfer but at least we did no harm to it and kept the troops out.

The Red Crescent doctors had had a troublesome six months of siege. The Turks stole most of their stores; the Albanians stalked them in the streets with intention of murder and robbery; two shells struck their house and another burst by the operating theatre of their hospital —apart from starvation there was fever, suspicion, and espionage. Between house and hospital they had been obliged to dodge from doorway to doorway.

The English House has a bath, perhaps the only bath in all Albania. It is of the old-fashioned sort, which was painted to look like a wild sort of marble, and had a lid. There is a pleasant picture remembered of Stathers of the Red Crescent taking his bath with the lid closed to keep out the shrapnel. Since in one certain minute of the bombardment forty shells came into the town (but this was the best time made) it was not unwise to take even that precaution.

For that night we slept on the floor of a room in the Hotel.

Scutari was quiet. There was no disorder, no looting, and no drinking. I did not see a drunk soldier from that night till we left.

Two barge-loads of bread arrived on the evening of the march in, and the loaves were distributed in the bazaar at once. Twice a day after that there was a distribution, a loaf for everyone, and on the third day lamps were put up for the first time in the town's history.

We breakfasted next morning on bacon and eggs, with plates and cups of pottery, a waiter, a table-cloth, looking-glasses all round, and a bill. The small pieces of siege bread, mahogany colour, hard as half dry putty and much coarser in grain, which was all they could get us before the morning distribution, with the crowd of child-beggars at the window, the hollow cheeks of the servants, and a pale clerk with his left arm shot away from the elbow, who was taking his coffee at the next table, were the only sights to remind us that anything uncommon had been going on.

One had the same impression sometimes on our own Shiroska mountain over Bobote—that it was more easy to fancy the country in deep peace than at war. From the outpost there, high up in clear wind, we used to watch the sheep browsing in Scutari meadows and a shepherd

. . the barber . . . was of two metres or so, very thin, aquiline, grave

or two sitting under a tree. The line of wire in the plain shone like a stream, it could be distinguished from water only by its shewing more blue and not changing colour with the sky. The gun emplacements were hidden in clumps of trees, the tents half buried in their pits behind the trench—they suggested at most the Tunbridge Wells cricket week, or a fair. This is not written or pretended for caprice—it is true that, what with the ordinary course of life being by the nature of man to seven-eighths of its consistency invariable and unchanging whatever you do, whether it is eel-fishing, flying, gambling, or polar-exploring, and what with the large indifference of hills, skies, sun, moon, and stars to small scuffles (the largest battle is small by comparison), it is by an imaginative effort rather than direct realisation that danger and the possibility of bullets can be understood. The sniper waits for the failure of the imagination and shoots you because you have forgotten that you must believe in him.

Lauder went away after breakfast to catch a returning bread-boat for Virpazar and so to Ireland. He had been more than a year campaigning, first with the Turks in Tripoli in a flat desert, then with the Montenegrins in a mountainous waste, and was tired of bad food, rags, lice, and hard lying. He strolled out of the war as he had come to it, and tied up its wounded and dosed its sick and walked about in its battles, with nonchalance—not the nonchalance of "don't-care," but of a level temper, a long endurance, a well-understood and well-liked profession, a friendly mind, and a sense of humour. He tilted his disreputable hat over his eyes, said, "Good-bye Doc, good-bye Cookee," asked me to keep an eye on the pup if she should be found, and walked away.

I went for a shave.

The Kiri river is made to run through the streets of Scutari new town in canals; a little bridge leads to each shop. The barber's shop was less than seven feet square and little higher than the barber, who was of two metres or so, very thin, aquiline, grave. He wore a white fez cut down to the size of a cabman's badge, and stuck miraculously on the back of a skull polled so close that it seemed to be bald, a white double-breasted waistcoat and tight white trousers piped with black braid. Between waistcoat and trousers was a foot of white shirt and six inches of red sash, in which a large silver mounted ramrod was stuck. I sat dangerously on a three legged chair with my feet through the door, overhanging the water, and held the shaving-dish, while he rubbed the soap on with his hand, and scraped off the beard with a knife like a small French cook's knife.

He then cut my hair until no hair could be seen at all, and went out to borrow a glass to shew me the results.

I marched off, very proud of a clean jaw and tidy head. Five Servian prisoners of the Brditza battle saluted in a row as I passed towards the bazaar.

The bazaar was crowded, though the booths were shut, and I could see a great crowd of troops and their flags on the slope of the castle-hill behind it. I asked a soldier of the Komerskozagaratchski whom I knew (he had carried a sack of dressings before the battle) what was happening. He told me that the keys were to be handed over by Essad this morning, and went with me through the mazes of the bazaar and up the hill. The Crown Prince's guard were at the gates, glorious in plumed black caps, red waistcoats, blue breeches, shining top-boots.

A few yards higher I found all our people in a group—Red Cross and Red Crescent together, with a mixture of the staff officers of both armies —standing at the edge of a small plateau beneath the castle keep. There was a tree in the middle of the plateau and under the tree a table at which sat Essad Pasha, a fat, fair man, and the Crown Prince Danilo, a square, dark man; both of middle age.

Essad's history is pretty well known—an Albanian by birth, and adventurer by calling, in which he has got on by successful assassination and a wise marriage. He is a son-in-law of Abdul Hamid, and rich.

The man who made the defence of Scutari possible was Hasan Riza Bey.

Danilo was on Bardanjoli as early as November of 1912, but left too small a garrison. Hasan drove them out and made Bardanjoli impregnable. He built also the great twelve mile line of redoubts and trenches from Muselim to the lake, which stopped the only level approach to Scutari.

When Hasan Riza was murdered, it was his officers that carried on the defence; Essad was not only incompetent but a coward.

He was made Commandant of Tarabos under Riza, but had to be sent back for running away in his first fight. He lived after the murder in the dungeons of the citadel and was never seen in the town. His orders were conveyed to the townspeople by the Austrian Consul and a certain well-known cut-throat—Suleiman Bey.

Suleiman shot a stretcher bearer in the open street, for jostling him. He must have had courage if all the stories of his murders are true—he was a better man than Essad.

The formal surrender did not take long. The keys passed from hand to hand and a paper or two were signed. The two Generalissimos shook hands and Danilo went up to the top of the bastion to see the flag hoisted. His guards were already drawn up, and a crowd of soldiers stood about. He made a short speech, the flag was sent up, the guard presented arms, the soldiers shouted, the guns fired a salvo, and the whole affair was over—we went back to lunch.

These sights with their colour and their interest, the old citadel, the worn soldiers and the sleek shining guard, the formal ending of a siege upon such a great stage of tumbling walls and clear skies, would have been impressive enough to anyone who had not seen that small figure walk out alone on the top of Tarabos. That moment was passionate, abrupt, and unforgettable, this, an anti-climax of formal ceremony and heel-clicking.

45

Dr. Goldsmith had come to Scutari in his own galley and took me back with him that afternoon. I was to bring in the kit and stores from Bobote. We travelled light with three sweeps out, and were three hours on the journey, an incomparable journey, in a cool sun, over smooth water.

Borjo and I climbed by the road called the Wounded's path, and each turn, stone, and rock of its three thousand feet up and two thousand down to Bobote again (for Bobote was on the mountain side, itself a thousand feet from the lower valleys) was separately known, even in the half dark.

Bobote was empty when we came to it; the whole country was empty. Round Bobote there was a small town of straw huts like bee-hives, in which the soldiers lived—and slept, heads to the wall, feet to the middle and the fire. At night each hut was lighted by its fire, the company lounged by the doorway in their long cloaks and sheepskins; sometimes one of them played on the one stringed lute and sang. The lute gave two notes; the song was always in falsetto, a monotonous chant of old family wars (each family has its songs; the families have their village; the village has its battalion) and loves and histories. When at night we came in from our marches, from Muričan over marshy valleys and downs full of thickets and thorns, from Oblique by every sort of country the fanciful world can shew, from Zogaj by the mountain, from Crepaj or Dramos, up and down the outpost road with Tarabos overlooking, generally hungry, footsore, and walking only by clockwork, the fires and straight rising smoke, the squatting groups among the rocks, the songs and gossip about the straw huts were our first gay foretaste of a comfortable civilization shortly to be realized round our own hearth, in stew, coffee, toe-toasting, relaxation of buttons on every side, pipes and bed in those pleasant sacks which cannot sting like the cold sheets of a demure respectability, or be kicked off, or fallen out of, or burst at the bottom, never leaky of draughts at the side, but as tight as the tucking-in of an only Prince by his Royal anxious mama, from their very nature, form, habit, and contriving.

Borjo and I lit our fire and fried our bread and bacon-fat, but it was the only fire and the only supper of ten deserted villages. It was more lonely than London on a Sunday, for that place is never more than a desert inhabited by wild animals while this had been a pleasant up and down land full of men.

We stumbled about the camp after supper with lanterns, but found not a soul. Borjo went as far as Vilgar and that was empty. The grenades, rifles, cartridges, and a few six inch shrapnel still lay in the stable under our room, but there was no one to guard them.

It was plain that no mules could be got nearer than Muričan. I made four packs of our blankets and a few medicinal stores worth keeping that night. I sent Borjo next morning for the mules, and set out myself towards the ridge. I climbed with the stolid indignation which was the only mood to carry one up that mountain, and did not stop even by that rock on the summit where everyone stopped to smoke and look about, but marched over the hills away from Vilgar, from Bobote, from Muričan, and all its downs and valleys, the paths, rocks, springs, hills, thickets between them, the shining loops of the Bojana, and the sea high up on the curve of the world.

It was with the back of my head that I saw all these things although my eyes were looking at the lake and Scutari, and beyond Scutari as far as motor-buses, with at least a glimpse of Zogaj and breakfast.

46

There had been three days' negotiation with Essad for the surrender —the principal terms were that his army was to be let march out by the Medua road with the field batteries; that each of the Turks should carry eight days' provisions, to be made up to that amount by the Montene-grins; that all the guns of position should be left in order with their ammunition.

A general assault was to take place at once if he refused these con-ditions, and while Essad knew that the town would fall, he was told he would be held personally responsible for any loss of life in such assault. Gurnić had sapped up to the last fort on Tarabos, Vukotić's trenches were within a hundred and fifty yards of the redoubts in the plain. The Turks had little ammunition left, and that mostly common shell, with food of the worst quality to last at furthest a week.

Meanwhile during those three days Cettinje was blockaded to pre-vent news from reaching Austria. It was known that Austria was ready to march. Austria is the Fee Fo Fum of South East Europe.

She is frightened by every Servian and Montenegrin success in case her own millions of Slav subjects should be encouraged to rebel. She has plenty of reason for anxiety. There was a Dalmatian battalion fight-ing for Montenegro, all Austrian subjects, all knowing that in every probability they could never get back to their own country. I met two Austrian corporals, who had run away to become private soldiers for King Nicholas.

When Doctor Sherwin, Todd, Starkie, and I were returning home, we stayed a day or two at Ragusa for the Brindisi boat.

The place was of course full of Austrian troops in war kit. The officers stopped us at every step for our passports, polite in manner, very rude in look. But when we went to bathe in the Tommies' bathing-place, we were received like brothers.

We had races and weight-lifting contests on the shore, they launched a canoe for Todd, and cheered loudly when after all he did not fall out of it. Of course they would have fought where and when they were told to, former inclination has not much to do with fighting when it starts, it provides its own incitements and passions, as anyone would discover who started a civil war in England, or a battle between two regiments even of the same division, but these soldiers were not in themselves enemies of the Serbs.

Austria sent as far as possible German-speaking troops or Magyars of the Serb frontiers (Serb includes Montenegrin) but Todd and Starkie found a Slav regiment on the Austrian side of Antivari bay, and the men were not only friendly to them and their cause, but inimical to Austria. They asked eagerly for news of the war, though always with precautions against the espionage of their non-commissioned officers, who were Germans, and they were delighted by the successes of the allies.

Austria has many agents in the Balkans, and the chief of them are the Catholic priests and friars. These she subsidizes, while Russia pays the priests of the Orthodox.

In Scutari the Austrian consul was Essad's close familiar. It was probably this man that prompted the murder of Hasan Riza Bey.

After the conference in London, when it was known that Turkey had surrendered claim to all except Adrianople, an old woman found her way through the investing lines into Scutari with a piece of newspaper in her shoe.

This paper shewed how far the allies had been successful, that relief by Turkish force was impossible, and that Scutari whomever she fell to, would never again be in the Ottoman power.

The paper passed quickly from hand to hand until Riza heard of it.

It is said that this determined him upon surrender. He had lost many of his best officers, he was a Turkish soldier, and found himself fighting, for what, he could not know, but certainly not Turkey—though the whole energy and success of the defence was due to him, he did not see why his men should risk their lives in the interests of Austria or a nebulous new state of Albania.

But he was shot in the street, coming from Essad's house, before he could make a decision, and the Austrian paid 2000 crowns for the paper.

Essad went to the dungeons of the castle for safety from Riza's soldiers, and with the consul's advice and for his bribes, continued the siege. It is possible they promised him the crown of new Albania.

In the same way the Austrian representative at Cettinje was the villain of the piece. I met him there at my first arrival. He was a dark, black haired, black moustached man, with eyes which had the look of being painted. I should say it was very likely that he did paint the edges of his lids, it certainly gave his expression a very truculent and romantic look. In the hotel (the only hotel) there is what is called the diplomatic table, where English, French, Russian, Servian, and the other Plenipotentiaries sat together in assumed good fellowship. This Austrian ate alone at another. He was only less secretive-looking, less like the hero of a novel by Le Queux, than some of the correspondents.

But he was able to tell me all about the operations, where the different divisions were, how many guns they had, when Austria would strike, and he was only at fault in the last.

He spoke English, and dined with me because he wished to exercise that tongue, and I was not a correspondent.

He had a big Fiat car in which he made long night drives. I suppose he could not have been prevented without an international incident— but there were not many things he did not know about the progress of the war.

During the negotiations for the surrender in May it was of course important to keep him from driving the few miles down to Cattaro, with the news. The blockade of Cettinje alone would warn him of developments, apart from the coming and going of the generals, and the rumours of the town.

Here is then a piece of typical Balkan politics—there is only one road over Lovchen to Cattaro and it was suddenly destroyed by a landslip. The landslip was in an upward direction according to the remains of it that I saw, and very local in its effect, destroying no more than ten yards or so of the top of a culvert. It was effected by dynamite, and the first news that reached Austria was of the surrender of Scutari, and the taking over by Montenegro of its almost impregnable forts.

Austria had her answer ready—she refused to pass the petrol for the King's cars through her customs, and she issued a police ordinance that no Montenegrin hack-cab was to come in by the Cattaro road (it was repaired with great speed two days after Scutari's fall) without a vet's certificate for the horses.

Her spies had informed her Foreign Office that there were no certified vets in Montenegro. The four or five old men who supported themselves by carrying travellers between Cettinje and Cattaro were hard hit by this counter stroke, and Count Berchtold had a diplomatic success.

I spent most of my days at the waterside . . . (opposite page) ·

47

I was rowed up the lake again that afternoon, taking a first load of stores, which was left in care of Marco the chief boatman, until carts could be got for the two miles journey between the waterside and the English House.

The rest of the party came in next afternoon with the rest of the stores, and Zogaj was also abandoned.

I spent most of my days at the waterside sitting on a stone and waiting for the carts.

There were seven of us in a row, three tribesmen crosslegged on their ankles, then a small child, then myself squatting, then two more small children. The children were worn out by the siege and listless with starvation. They sat with perfectly blank looks and did not speak or move at all, except for an occasional blink towards the sun. The Ghegs talked politics and rolled cigarettes. I lit a pipe and watched the boats of the refugees going home. Their baggage included all sorts of strange things, plush sofas, French gilt chairs, I saw even a dumb-waiter in one boat that held nothing else but rags, hoes, spades, and children.

The whole of that end of the lake was in movement. The bridge carried two long files, one of fugitives going, the other of soldiers coming in with the guns; there was a camp opposite, all between were the boats little and big, tracing in and out as if in a complicated minuet; the sky was full of small running clouds, and their shadows raced up the backs of the mountains like a storming party, dipping into the dark blue of a gully for cover, flying over a bluff in open order as if they could hear bullets.

When after two hours Marco came for a bread-order to be signed, I found myself in a sort of trance. One child had gone to sleep with his head in my lap—I seemed to have filled and lit a pipe recently, for it was stuck in my teeth and throwing up a good cloud of smoke—my coat and shirt were unbuttoned and stood open, whereas at my last recollection they had been all taut.

I wrote my name on the order with the back of the small child's skull for my desk (he did not wake), cocked my hat a little further over my eyes, moved my seat an inch or two to avoid soreness, and returned shortly to whatever inner cave of being that is where pipes are lit, children nursed, and coats opened unhelped by the intelligence. Suddenly (but it was an hour after) the bullocks appeared in front of me cooling their legs in the water. I daresay they had stood there fifteen minutes before the large white island they made between the caïques attracted my dazed eye. I laid the child on a sack and dived at once into the crowd to catch the carters. They were squatting on the shore smoking cigarettes. They made a bustle of departure that waked all the loungers of the quay and fitted well into the hurry of the water and the sky. The politicians were moved from their ankles to carry boxes, the children put off the footway with a loaf of bread for consideration, the bullocks brought to land by a boat with howls and sticks.

The bazaar was now pretty near impassable with crowds. The tribes all seemed to have come to town together with all their women, and each woman with a cradle on her back. The only wide street was blocked by the big guns, dragged each by a hundred or so soldiers. My carts were generally under arrest; as soon as I left one to itself to release the other, the first was stopped. The dust, heat, noise, and jostling were beyond telling.

The booths were again open and each one had a crowd before it. In each one too there was a ceremonious party sitting cross-legged on the counter over their coffee cups. They smoked a cigarette or two, then drank their coffee at a gulp and began on another cigarette while another brew was made. Here and there, there was a Montenegrin soldier walking hand in hand with his wife, a farmer riding his shaggy hill pony, an Albanian chief stiff with gold braid and a high pedigree.

Marcović came riding by and stopped to talk for five minutes while my way was blocked by a gun. Essad he told me was supposed to have joined forces with Djavid Pasha from Janina, near Valona, and trouble was expected.

He asked me if I could stay if the Austrians came and there was a second siege.

"When are they expected?" I asked.

"Tonight or tomorrow, mon cher, or never at all."

Marcović has a habit of saying "mon cher" after every phrase when he stops to find a construction for the next.

He was floored by a subjunctive after four "mon chers," and rode off on the fifth with a wave of the hand.

The carters cried "Haidé!" and flourished their goads, the bullocks dropped their heads and rolled their eyes, the wheels creaked forward.

The last note I have is that morning's, reading:

Fetch stores from quay, thirty-seven pieces—and Lauder's bed—two carts.

The Austrians did not come, as you know, and there is nothing more to write. We stayed ten days in Scutari, mainly to look at the Turkish forts, and had an easy journey back to beef-steaks by way of Bari and Naples.

If this proves a disappointing book it must be because there is too much eating, and too little incident in it—too much like life, which is perhaps disappointing for the same reason.

NOTES

I. This is the list of the medical stores brought by Ogilvie to Rjeka
The Drugs

Dover's Powder	gr.V
Pil Ipecac c Scilla	gr.IV
Pil Plumbi c Opio	gr.IV
Pil Col et Hyos	gr.IV
Aspirin	gr.X
Pot. Chlorate tablets	gr.X
Quinine Sulphate	gr.V

B 2 W Hyd Perchlor
2 Pot iod Tabloids
Hypodermics
Morphine Tartrate
Strychnine
Eucaine lactate
Antiseptics
Hyd. Perchlor
Biniodide
Pure Carbolic
Pure Iodine
Dressings
Compressed wool
Bandages
Cyanide gauze
Lint
Gutta Percha tissue
Yellow mercury ointment.

With a Liniment made by ourselves of eggs, olive oil, turpentine and vinegar, Rjeka was doctored as it had never been before. The Practice extended ten miles over the mountains in every direction before the end of the war. Doctoring of any sort, but especially free doctoring, appeals strongly to all rustic peoples. Of course the Red Cross was not in Montenegro to look after the general public—but when the wounded and sick of the army were dressed it would have been hard to refuse their fathers, brothers, wives, sons, and daughters. Both Ogilvie and Dobson worked from ten to fourteen hours a day always, and were almost held ready for canonization by the people about. If they had drunk even all the cognacs which they were offered in a day apart from wine, coffee, flowers, oranges, they would both have had hobnailed livers in a week. Many patients had to be removed from the hospital by force (the Governor, a kind fellow of six feet seven in height, was generally sent for to terrorise them) in order to be passed on to Cettinje or Podgoritza, where the base hospitals were.

When Ogilvie joined the Servians at Medua in December of 1912, his fame (by way of patients returned to fight) was there already; so that the whole staff of both armies insisted on dining with him every night, to the embarrassment of his equipment and the proving of Joe Baverstock, who far excelled anything that had before been thought possible to be done with beans, bacon-fat, bully, and rice.

II. Hasan Riza constructed a line of wire with circular forts (I think seven) at regular intervals across the plain between the hills and the lake to the North West of Scutari.

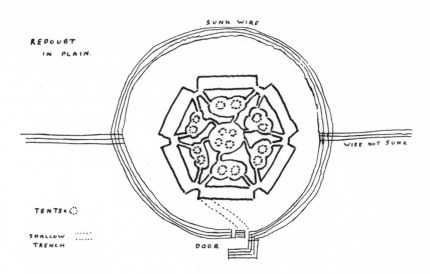

I give a sketch of them and of the Montenegrin approach trenches. These were pushed up to within a hundred and fifty yards at the time of the surrender.

At first the experiment was made of rolling large cylinders over the fields in front of the Montenegrin pioneers to cover this work. These consisted of a case of thin iron and an inner shell of wicker, with cement between.

Bullets of course had to penetrate both sides and the air-space in the middle in order to do any damage. A pompom would have stopped them but shrapnel was no good. In the end they came too close to be handled without exposing their crews, who were besides open on each flank to rifle fire. They are probably not so good an expedient as the portable shield, the sort of thing used by the Servians at Adrianople (I believe the Bulgars have them too—the French police use them against anarchists—a form was tried by our own War Office some years ago but has not since been heard of) which is more handy if not quite so stout. As you see, the approaching trench was cut in a succession of traverses or buttresses. The sappers crawled forward each night and threw up four or five or half a dozen small mounds one in front of the other. Under cover of these and in and out between them the trench was dug during the day—they became the tops of the traverses.

The Montenegrins however were in too much of a hurry to get to close quarters and began in a very short time to set their mounds too far apart. Instead of the trench advancing in this manner

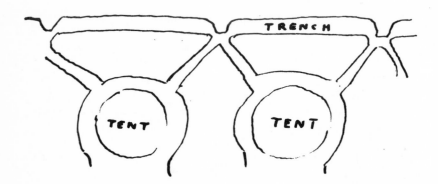

it went like this

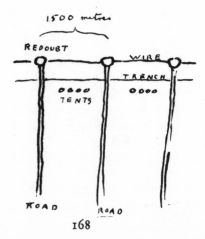

with the result that shrapnel and rifle shot got easily into it, and they lost many men that might have been saved.

It is noticeable that the Turks on Bardanjoli, where the trenches were very well made, deep, clean, and extremely narrow, avoided the necessity of frequent traverses, which not only increase the work but make the trenches harder to get about in, by putting at intervals a couple of iron bars (posts for barbed wire) across the top and piling two or three feet of sacks on them.

This made almost as effective (as effective or more than the old-fashioned bonnet of fortification) a protection from enfilading as a traverse, and did not block the trench.

SECTION OF GLACIS AND BOMBPROOF

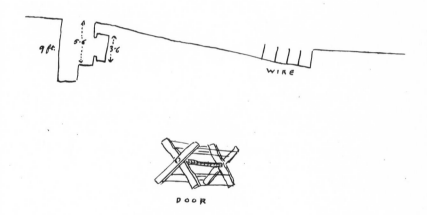

DOOR

The sacks of course were small in size as sacks should be.

The difference between the Montenegrin and Turkish gun positions was noticeable. The Turks relied on the natural dips and hills of the ground to hide their guns, while the Montenegrins built emplacements of stones or dug them out deep enough to protect the gun.

They chose a commanding mountain, hauled their guns up it, and placed them as high as they could.

The Turks kept behind the mountains as a rule, and fired over them.

This is what the Montenegrin gun positions on Shiroska looked like.

169

[Sketch missing.] The mountain should be larger, the positions less conspicuous, but they were quite conspicuous enough.

On Tarabos proper were no guns (except of course maxims), they were on the plateau behind, and there they stood practically in the open. This was the arrangement:

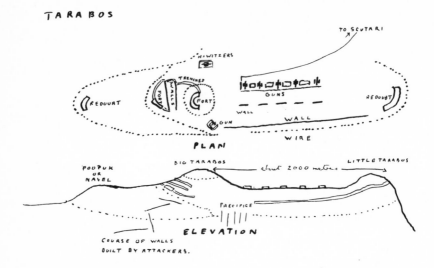

It should be explained that there was no parapet in front of the gun. It could be turned in any direction, nor were the pits very deep, little higher than the hubs of the wheels.